A SLOW GOODBYE

Nightmare Whispers Forged into a Story

RAMONA STOIAN

*"We all have had or will have our deaths.
It is disturbing to know that we only think they are dead,
but they continue to be near us, to hear us, to see us..."*

(Dumitru Constanin Dulcan)

I

Elira found herself in a perplexing confluence of relentless sorrow, tragedy, and a bitter unknown. The question nagged at her like an unyielding riddle. How had she ended up there? Yet, deep down, she understood that the answer eluded her grasp, perhaps forever out of reach in this life.

She was not one to embark on peculiar nocturnal escapades, especially far from the comforts of home. The darkness wrapped around her like a veil, and an unsettling sense of solitude clung to her. Memories of how she had arrived in this desolate place remained shrouded in a haze, like elusive specters. Confusion reigned as she couldn't decipher whether she was wet or cold. She looked around, her surroundings an eerie tableau of another world, a macabre Earth. The air was thick with fog, raindrops fell like tears from a mournful sky, and the ground beneath her feet exuded a feeling of desolation. Unparalleled thoughts and emotions swirled within her mind. A disorienting maelstrom left her trembling with fear.

The darkened street stretched before her, caught in a liminal space between the city and the ring road. Lights and distant buildings tantalized her, so near yet impossibly far away. A faintly illuminated bus station stood like a lonely sentinel, its emptiness at this late hour an enigma that added to her growing sense of disconnection. Even though the place was recognizable by its physical features, a strange conviction crept over her; this was not the Earth as she knew it. She pondered the surreal possibility of not feeling the rain as droplets fell around her. Strangely, the icy bite of the night failed to register in her body. It was as if sensations had become secondary, overshadowed by a sinister awareness of her thoughts and emotions, an unexplainable detachment from her physical self.

"Please, just be patient. This will all be over soon," said a voice.

Elira's eyes widened in recognition. "Oh my God, Teo! Hi, hi... Teo, why are we here? How did we end up here? I, I, I..." Her words faltered. Her best friend, Teo, stood there with concern, even though tranquility shadowed her eyes.

"Do you want to see the real world, Elira?" Teo asked gently. "I can show you. Come with me."

"I don't understand. Go where?" Elira replied, her confusion deepening.

Mystery covered the moment, leaving Elira both troubled and intrigued. Without warning, as if summoned by the uncertainty of their situation, they found themselves at the deserted bus station. Silence dominated, broken only by the distant echo of the darkness.

Suddenly, a bus screeched to a halt before them. Its imposing presence was almost otherworldly in that dimly lit station. The middle door swung open with a nagging squeak, revealing an impenetrable black. Elira's heart raced as she cautiously peered inside, her curiosity and trepidation intensifying.

A figure emerged from the shadows, like a revelation —a figure she had never expected to see in that strange place. Her mother, Liv, was stepping out of the bus with inexplicable secrecy and an inscrutable expression.

The tension was palpable, as if the bus station itself held the answers to the myriad questions that had haunted Elira. Her mother's presence, in such a peculiar manner, only deepened the mysteries that had entangled their lives.

Elira's head spun, and her thoughts fragmented like shards of glass. Her memory had gaps, missing pieces in a puzzle that refused to come together.

"How can this be possible?" Elira muttered to herself, her voice quivering with uncertainty. She desperately needed clarity, but she was trapped in confusion. In this inexplicable setting, the reunion with her mother plunged Elira into an entirely new abstruse state.

She thought her mom was...

Confronted with the odd, she couldn't rely on her recollection of events. The past few days had wiped clean, leaving a void in her memory. She had no alternative but to trust her instincts, following the signals in her emotions like breadcrumbs guiding her through the convoluted twister of life. Staring at her mother, whose presence defied all logic, Elira finally gathered the courage to speak.

"Mom, what are you doing here?" Elira asked, her words tinged with fear and curiosity. "Why are you barefoot?" she continued.

Elira's attention remained fixed on her mother, a spectral figure draped in an elegant, flowing white garment that seemed to cascade like moonlight. Liv's unshod feet made no sound as they met the ground. A silent lament emanated from her, enveloping Liv in an unfathomable melancholy. Her voice, it seemed, was held hostage. Lost. Pain.

It was not a pain of the flesh; it was something far more arcane, buried deep within her being. Elira, like a seer, sensed the agony that gripped her mother's soul and permeated the air around them. The knowledge that some nameless affliction dominated her mother had been with Elira since childhood, a mystery unsolved for years.

Yet, in this unnatural revelation, her mother defied her suffering. She stood there, a paradox of beauty and despair. Liv's strength transcended the sadness that clung to her like a haunting melody. It was a silent symphony, a secret only they could hear, binding mother and daughter in a cryptic dance of life and mystery, where the answers remained buried in the shadows.

Elira's heart was trapped in a vise as if something strong was about to grab and squeeze it—a vast invisible hand that wrung her heart with supernatural powers. She screamed and howled inside. All she wanted was to cry. The intense perception that something terrible would happen made her return to thinking and search for a solution—a solution for the unknown—a way out!

"Teo, what did you mean by real world? Where do you want to go? Please call a taxi. Help me in this, would you?" Desperate, Elira asked. But Teo was staring blankly without any response.

Somehow, the rain stopped, and Elira couldn't remember exactly when or how she got barefoot. Then she looked at Teo's feet; oddly, she was wearing only pink and dry socks, no shoes. The dawn was breaking, and her mom pointed to the nearby hill.

With time slipping away like grains of sand through her trembling fingers, Elira held to her last glimmer of hope, a desperate search for any means of transportation. Her heart raced, and her mind raced even faster as she scanned the dark streets for a car, a taxi, a bus—any way to take her mother home. The frightening presence of the hill sent shivers down her spine. It was an ominous place she dreaded to explore.

Elira's mother had expressed an unspoken desire to visit her parents, a journey laden with complex emotions. Through an inexplicable thought floating like a vapor in her mind, Elira knew her mother wasn't welcome there. Not just yet.

On the eastern side of the city rests a solitary hill, a silent sentinel guarding a secret treasure. At the foot of this timeless mound, a small village lay in slumber. It was where time had seemingly stood still, a place that held the promise of becoming a fantastic tourist attraction.

Its untamed beauty should have drawn visitors from far and wide, but a series of challenges conspired to keep it hidden, veiled in obscurity. The primary obstacle was the condition of its streets. The passage of countless seasons had etched their toll, rendering the paths uneven and treacherous. These ancient roads, though picturesque in their own right, posed a formidable barrier to curious travelers, discouraging them from venturing deeper into the heart of the village.

Another more intangible challenge was the villagers' demeanor. While they were the custodians of this living time capsule, their reserved nature and, at times, aloofness created an invisible barrier that kept visitors at arm's length. Warmth and friendliness, the essence of hospitality, were in short supply.

The villagers held the key to breathing life into their beloved hamlet. The winds of change whispered the need for genuine smiles and open arms. Perhaps some places were destined to defy the march of time and the tide of transformation.

That place would remain a stubborn outlier, a testament to the resilience of tradition and the unyielding spirit of its inhabitants. And so, as the world moved forward, this little corner would remain steadfastly rooted in its peculiar ways.

At the village's entrance was a beautiful Orthodox church standing slightly away from the first house. It was a place of profound spiritual significance for the villagers, and Elira's grandmother made it a point to lead her there every Sunday. A church, a symbol of tradition and devotion, that held a remarkable secret within its sacred confines.

The church ceiling was decorated with a fresco painting, a masterpiece of illusionism, representing the sacrifice of Isaac, where an angel keeps Abraham from sacrificing his son, as God had asked him to do as a test of his faithfulness. It was amazing how Isaac's eyes were painted. So realistic! No matter where you sat in the church, he always looked at you.

One day, after the Divine Liturgy, little Elira started to run from one corner to the other of the church, looking up to the ceiling to connect with Isaac. He was no ordinary friend. He was neither imaginary nor real but rather an enigmatic presence that had captured Elira's heart and imagination. After all, she had met him for a reason, and since that fateful day, he had become an inseparable part of her life.

As Elira continued to run, her chestnut curls bouncing with each step, Isaac followed her every move. He was a specter of some kind, an ethereal figure dancing upon the periphery of her vision, yet always within reach. His form was ever-shifting, like a mirage born from the interplay of light and shadow, and he moved with a grace that transcended the earthly realm.

Elira's fascination with Isaac knew no bounds. To her, he was a ray of enchantment, a portal to a dimension where the impossible was not only possible but embraced. In her mind, he was the embodiment of magic, and their connection was the stuff of dreams.

With each turn, each twirl, Elira felt the boundaries of her world blur and bend. The once-solid ceiling seemed to stretch and contort as if reaching to touch her outstretched fingers. The edges of reality dissolved, and a big picture of wonder and whimsy unfurled in their place.

In that sacred solitude, where the echoes of prayers and the scent of incense still clung to the air, Elira and Isaac danced. They danced around the celestial patterns that adorned the ceiling, their spirits intertwined in a waltz of the heart and soul. In that timeless moment, the ordinary became extraordinary, transforming the mundane into the miraculous.

And so, in the soul of the empty church, beneath the watchful eyes of the saints depicted in the frescoes, Elira and Isaac wove their own tale of magic and wonder. With each passing second, their connection deepened, and they found a unique bond in the soft, golden light that filtered through the stained glass.

Sunday after Sunday, the routine repeated itself. Week after week, Elira found herself trudging along the dusty path, her little feet struggling to keep pace with her grandmother's determined stride. They journeyed to church, a holy pilgrimage that had become as much a part of their lives as the changing seasons. At some point, Elira's youthful exuberance waned, replaced by a growing sense of fatigue and curiosity.

The road from home to church was long, and they had to walk most of the way. It was exhausting for both of them, but her grandmother never uttered a word of complaint.

Elira had very little free time to spend with her friends, explore games of childhood, or chase her dreams under the open sky. She only had one day of the week to play, and unfortunately, on that same day, she had to accompany her grandmother to the church. She was either in school or had to do homework for the rest of the week.

In the tangle of her child's mind, Elira couldn't help but ponder the idea that her grandmother was engaged in a solemn act of sacrifice. Many questions weighed heavily on her young heart.

Why suffer this way when there are other options today? Did God require such sacrifices? Would God stop loving them if they attended a different church? Elira couldn't fathom why love and devotion to God would be bound to the specific walls of a single church. She couldn't understand how her grandmother never complained about the arduous trek.

Innocently or not, she believed that God should love them anyway, regardless of where they worshipped. After all, doesn't God forgive their sins, guiding them to Heaven? Elira found solace in these thoughts, the comforting belief that God's love was boundless and unconditional.

In her contemplation, a flicker of insight began to dawn. What if her grandmother's commitment to their Sunday adventure was not solely about religious devotion? What if, beneath it all, her grandma simply wanted to spend more time sharing precious moments with her beloved granddaughter?

The idea settled in Elira's heart like a warm embrace. She realized that her grandmother's love was a guiding force that compelled her to pilgrimage to the hillside church, week after week. The grasp brought a newfound sense of gratitude and understanding.

Rather than risk upsetting her grandma with questions and doubts, Elira accepted their Sunday tradition gracefully. She understood that there were more important reasons than she had initially grasped, and her grandma's love was the compass that led the way.

Two significant reasons gave her the strength to keep walking up that hill. The love—unconditional love. And Isaac. His presence brought a touch of magic to Elira's life, a connection to something much more powerful. He was a source of fascination and wonder, a reminder that there was more to the world than met the eye.

Elira's faith began to evolve, shaped not only by her grandma's devotion but also by her growing understanding of love and the enduring magic of belief. Going to the church was not an obligation but a shared act of care that strengthened their relationship and connected them to something greater than themselves.

As the sun painted the sky in hues of gold and crimson on another Sunday, Elira walked beside her grandmother, her steps more purposeful, her heart lighter. The questions in her mind were not gone, but they no longer weighed her down. With Isaac by her side, Elira knew their spiritual and personal expedition was worth traveling.

Of course, Elira's grandmother knew what was on her mind. While all grandmothers have an extraordinary intuition, Elira's was even more remarkable. With a gentle smile and a loving gaze, she decided it was time to offer an explanation.

Elira's grandmother shared a valuable lesson. "Faith is not the same as religion." Her words, filled with wisdom and experience, were delivered with kindness. There was no judgment or reproach in her tone, only a gentle reminder of the difference between the two.

Not just a response but also a revelation. They cut through the confusion and illuminated the path forward for her young mind. It was like one sentence had unlocked a door to an ocean of understanding.

All the pieces came together seamlessly. There were clear distinctions between God, faith, respect, tradition, and moral values.

Religion was a structured framework in which people expressed their faith, while faith itself was the firm belief that beat all limits and doctrines.

As a river discovering its path, a sense of clarity overwhelmed her. She comprehended that her exploration and understanding journey was far from over, but she had found a guiding light. Her grandmother's words opened a new chapter of true meaning, compassion, and appreciation for the complexities of faith and spirituality.

Looking deeply into her grandmother's eyes, she felt grateful for the invaluable wisdom imparted. She had gained a better point of view and admiration of religion. Elira believed in the existence of one God for all, but she was still fascinated by the various ways in which people worshipped. It stumped her why other religions were considered taboo at school and home. Therefore, she decided to explore the mystery of religion, digging into the perspective of understanding, searching for reasonable answers, and chasing the power of belief.

Elira's grandmother had a cherished purpose for introducing her to the age-old village church. To her, it was a sanctuary of subtle teachings.

The people gathered there were not just Sunday service attendees; they were deeply devoted souls who carried themselves with a sense of dignity that reflected their reverence for the sacred. Immaculately dressed and well-mannered, they embodied a timeless tradition of respect. Their simple attire was a manifestation of their inner devotion.

The women were standing in front of their Creator, dressed in long skirts that brushed against the worn stone floor. Their heads were covered with soft scarves or modest headbands, and they wore no makeup or artificial embellishments. However, their natural beauty shone from within, pure, simple, and undeniable.

The churchgoers' behavior was not imposed by a rigid rule; it was instead a personal choice. They saw the church as a sacred space where they shed the superficial trappings of the world and adorned themselves with humility. This way of conduct spoke volumes about their reverence for the Lord's house.

At the beginning of the service, another display of devotion was revealed. The men and women present were seated separately, with men on the right side of the church and women on the left. This was not a result of discrimination or prejudice; instead, it was a practice rooted in faith for centuries. The purpose of this separation was to eliminate temptations, allowing the congregation to fully immerse themselves in prayer.

Through this significant action, they symbolized a commitment to a deeper connection with the Divine, unencumbered by worldly distractions. It was a practice that echoed through generations, a powerful reminder that their spiritual journey was intensely personal and that, within the hallowed walls of the church, they came together to seek solace, wisdom, and grace.

At this place, Elira learned about the significance of reverence, devotion, and the timeless traditions that bind the human soul to something greater than oneself. It was an insight into a world where faith, respect, and ethic are interwoven to create a devotion that transcends time and speaks to the essence of the human spirit.

Where the village ends, at the foot of the hill, after the last house - the abandoned house, there is a small path surrounded by groves leading to a cemetery. The Sorrowful Path!

The dilapidated house, a relic of a past era, stood guard at the entrance to the railway. Its windows were shattered, and the roof sagged under years of neglect. It was said that the house was cursed, and its former occupants had disappeared mysteriously one by one, leaving behind nothing but creepy tales and unanswered questions. But it was just a story to scare the kids fooling around. The people who inhabited the residence passed away from natural causes, and no one ever laid claim to the property. Or did they?

A narrow pathway, barely wide enough for two people to walk side by side, wound through a dense and tangled thicket of trees and overgrown bushes. It appeared to remain in a constant state of twilight, almost as if the sun's rays were too afraid to breach the darkness that enveloped it.

The cemetery at the end of the line was a place of quiet contemplation shrouded in fog. Weathered and moss-covered tombstones stood like sentinels; their inscriptions faded with time. It was a place where the departed rested in eternal slumber, their stories hidden beneath the Earth. Some said that the cemetery was full of secrets, that if you listened closely, you could hear the whispers of the dead, sharing tales of love and betrayal, of joy and despair.

Despite its unsettling reputation, the cemetery was a corner of pity for some. The mourners who came to pay their respects found comfort in the hilltop's stillness, the rustling of leaves, and the distant echoes of their footsteps as they walked along the Sorrowful Path. For in that quiet solitude, they felt a connection to the past and a reminder of the fleeting nature of life itself.

It's best to leave some secrets undisturbed, as the veil between the living and the dead is thin.

"Teo, can you please help me find a taxi? Please, please! We need to go home now! Something doesn't feel right with my mom, with me...with us. Please!" Elira pleaded, her confusion growing. "Mom, please talk to me! Why are you crying? Why do you want to go there?" She continued to implore, but neither of them responded.

Time seemed to slip away, and Liv's condition deteriorated. She was changing, her face growing pale, and Elira feared losing her again. "Teo, give me your socks."

Yelling at Teo, Elira continued, "Who are you? I don't recognize you at all. You drive me crazy. We're going home, with or without your help."

"No, darling, no! We're not going home. Not now," Teo replied nervously, tears streaming down her face. "They're all there, waiting for us. Come on, don't make it more difficult. Your mom wants this, too. She wants to go to the hill."

The strange experience of the circumstances continued

as Elira struggled to resolve the mystery surrounding their destination and her mother's inexplicable desire. Elira keenly sensed her mother's yearning to climb the hill, a desire that seemed almost magnetic in its pull.

Out of the question! Returning home was non-negotiable now, even for Teo.

Elira was determined to confront the apparent madness ahead and refused to give in to the chaos that would ensue if they continued. It was a battle of wills and a test of her perseverance, but she remained steadfast in her determination. She understood that giving in to the allure of the hill would only result in disorder and confusion. She would stand her ground to maintain order in their bewildering predicament, which was the only way.

II

Teo was a captivating woman with a unique charm. Her lustrous black hair framed her face like a cascade of silk, and her remarkable self-assuredness radiated from within, making her a compelling presence. She possessed striking and hypnotic beauty that drew people's attention wherever she went. Elira considered Teo to be her closest and dearest friend.

The two women had been inseparable since college. They shared a special friendship that was destined from the start. Their lively spirits were contagious, bringing happiness to everyone around them.

Teo had an exceptional organizational talent, ensuring that every detail fell perfectly into place. Her ability to plan with precision and finesse often left others in awe. Whether it was coordinating memorable outings or managing study sessions, she possessed an uncanny knack for making everything run seamlessly.

Life is full of changes that affect everyone, including Teo. Over time, she encountered numerous challenges and transformations, but she handled them gracefully, just as she had always done. Despite these shifts in her life, Teo remained a constant source of positivity.

Teo's vibrant spirit seemed to have faded over time, leaving a lingering sense of nostalgia that enveloped her like a gentle mist. She was no longer the exuberant soul who once effortlessly charmed everyone at college parties, the girl who had brightened up every room with her magnetic presence. She often retreated into her thoughts, replacing her once dynamic personality with a more introspective one.

She firmly believed that conversation was the solution to every problem. Teo had unwavering faith in the power of words. However, despite her inclination to engage in meaningful conversations and gain profound insights, her life contradicted this belief. She found herself trapped in a labyrinth of her own thoughts, unable to find answers to the questions that plagued her.

It was a strange turn of events that the very thing she had advocated for, the importance of communication and dialogue, appeared inadequate in calming the burdens of her own existence.

Teo's transformation showed the complexity of the human spirit and served as a reminder that even the most charismatic individual could be affected by sadness. She found herself in an unhappy marriage where love still existed, but circumstances blocked it. Her husband, a man she had once believed would love and cherish her unconditionally, had grown distant and indifferent. He either no longer knew how to appreciate her, or worse, he knew but simply didn't care.

As Teo crossed through this new phase of her life, she devoted herself to reading, thinking, and pondering. While her philosophy remained unshaken, she couldn't help but wonder if the answers she sought were not hidden in conversations with her husband but in the quiet moments of self-reflection, exploring the depths of her feelings.

A year after graduating, Teo's life changed when she fell in love and married. Their union was perfect—until it wasn't.

As time passed, the shine of their love started to fade away. Teo's husband began to slip away from their relationship. It all started innocently, with a harmless interest in gambling, but it quickly spiraled into an all-consuming addiction. No matter how hard Teo tried to help him, her efforts failed. She remained steadfast by his side, always there when he needed her, refusing to abandon him —unless he chose to leave her.

With a touch of naivety, she waited for the day he might ask for a divorce. But he was so deeply entrenched in their life together that he would never choose that way. Perhaps faith will choose for them. *Or not!*

A potential new love interest could displace him, but he loved Teo and couldn't imagine life without her, even though addiction had taken precedence.

Sometimes, Teo had moments where she felt like her old self again. Those moments only happened when she was around her best friend, Elira. Their conversations reignited Teo's enthusiasm, especially when Elira shared her unusual dreams. Teo felt like a paranormal detective in Elira's orbit.

Elira was a great friend who found herself caught in the middle of the troubled relationship between Teo and her husband. She was also close to Teo's husband, which gave her a unique perspective on their union. Elira had always wanted the best for her friends and had a fervent desire to see them overcome and once again experience the warmth of happiness.

Elira was grappling with the question of whether love is stronger than addiction or any other force or if it is merely a product of the imagination. She had witnessed the connection between Teo and her husband firsthand, observing moments of laughter and tenderness that had once characterized their love.

Still holding onto hope, Elira was convinced that love could change even the most lost souls toward redemption. Yet, the question remained: Was it strong enough to overcome the seductive pull of addiction?

For she knew that true love, when tested, had the strength to weather any tempest, and perhaps, it would prove to be the signal that guided them back to each other's arms.

III

Elira was tormented by her inability to comprehend Teo's behavior. Was her friend insane, or could she not come to terms with the truth?

"We will go home, darling, but first, we must take care of Liv. Everyone is waiting for us. We must go to the hill. We only have a little time left. We have to bury her."

The final two words surged into Elira's consciousness, igniting a disorienting whirlwind. Faith's sharp blade pierced her soul as an unsettling revelation unfolded: her mother was very alive. At that very moment! How, in the name of the Universe, could someone condemn another to the depths of a living burial?

Nonsense, sadness, bitterness, tears, confusion. Was this present real and unreal at the same time? Was the world she lived in both real and unreal? It had been a complicated paradox. Or madness!

Resolute in her determination, Elira wouldn't surrender. With a firm grasp on Liv's hand, she set her course for the city, compelling Teo to follow them. They were bound for home; come what may, nothing could stand in her way.

Lost in her thoughts, Elira failed to perceive that Liv was, in reality, guiding them up the hill, to the path known as the Sorrowful Path. The shadow of home was a distant mirage.

They pressed onward inexorably as Elira's mother's grip remained firm, forcing her to follow without the power to resist. Elira's body seemed to act like a marionette under her mother's control, her every movement devoid of her own will from the outset.

"Oh God! This is real!" said Elira astonished.

Once they reached the abandoned house in the village, Elira began to realize that the cemetery was the final destination. Her mom wanted to go there. The paranormal power she had to force her daughter to walk and control her movements was strong enough to prove how badly she wanted to be with her parents, both buried there.

The grave was now visible, surrounded by family members, with the priest sitting at the end of it. Many people were there, waiting for Liv, waiting for the funeral to begin.

"In the name of the Father, and of the Son, and of the Holy Spirit. Amen," the priest paused momentarily and looked at Liv, silently inviting her to get into the coffin. "I will not die but live, and I will proclaim what the Lord has done," he paused once more before continuing. This is the day the Lord has made; let us rejoice and be glad in it."

Reciting from the Bible, the priest focused on the mother and daughter. His expression was a mix of sorrow for Elira and happiness for Liv. As the verses filled the air, Elira's composure began to crumble. The unique circumstances and the contrasting emotions within the small gathering combined to push her to the edge.

Elira's heart ached with a profound, agonizing pain that cut deeper than any physical wound. As she sat at the funeral, surrounded by mourners, her mother's presence was a bittersweet agony that gnawed at her soul. She clutched her mother's hand, feeling the very essence of her existence, and yet, the sight of the casket was an unbearable weight on her chest.

The incongruity of the situation was a relentless assault on her emotions, tearing at the core of her reality. The thought of her mother, so vividly alive right next to her, being confined to that lifeless box was a persecution she could scarcely endure. It was a pain that transcended the physical and delved deep into the depths of her heart, leaving her emotionally torn and bewildered.

Every heartbeat pulsed with the strain of an indescribable tension, and as the funeral procession moved forward, Elira's inner unrest became more intense. She longed for answers, for a resolution to a strange and heart-wrenching paradox that had engulfed her life.

"Mom, let's run away from this place. Mom, please don't leave me. Please, Mom, stay, live...." Elira started to beg in tears. She was demolished and, at the same time, angry with herself. As a competent woman who could deal with anything life threw at her, she was now unable to manage anything.

Overwhelmed by the torrent of emotions, Elira couldn't hold back any longer. She fell to her knees, clasping her mother's hand and pleading with her not to enter the coffin. Tears streamed down her cheeks as she repeated the agonizing question, "Why? Why can't I save you, Mom?"

She glanced around the gathering, each familiar face seemingly unaffected by the surreal scene. Her father, Teo, her friends, and most notably, Nick, her boyfriend, all stood there, their impassive expressions mirroring her mother's inexplicable fate.

Elira's voice quivered as she cried out to them, her desperation echoing through the hushed cemetery. "You people see she's alive! Why you don't help me? Why?"

The pain. Indescribable. Endless. In a world of profound emotions and complex human connections, an unspoken bond exists between a mother and her child. It's a bond where a mother can sense her child's greatest emotions, the deepest burn.

Kissing her daughter tenderly on the forehead, that mother made a decision that would end the harrowing ordeal that had gripped them both.

"My child, I am dead," she whispered softly, her voice carrying a weight of resignation and love. "I must go now."

With those poignant words, the world around them dissolved into darkness. It was as if the air had been sucked away, leaving Elira in a void of emptiness. In that haunting moment, she could recall everything—the bittersweet memories, the laughter, the shared secrets, and the love they had once shared.

Her mother's departure left an indelible mark on her heart, a painful reminder of her irreplaceable loss. She remembered everything!

IV

At seven minutes past seven in the morning, Elira was awoken by pots and pans clattering in the kitchen. As she opened her eyes, she realized that it had all been a dream. She blinked and tried to shake off the remnants of the dream that still remained in her mind. Elira sometimes believed in science and thought that dreams could be messages from the subconscious that reveal essential issues, such as stress. Other times, she didn't know what to believe.

Lying in bed, she was overwhelmed by a sense of grief, as if her mother had been dead. It was a disturbing sensation, like a puzzle piece that refused to fit into the bigger picture of her life. As she dreamt, a part of her recognized the uneasy feeling that this dream could be a forewarning of some kind - a communication from her subconscious or a whisper from the Universe. However, another part of her, a voice created from skepticism and fear, tried to persuade her that the dream meant nothing. But the details were etched into her mind like an animated painting, each sharp and clear. It felt like her mind had carefully crafted a message inscribed in the unknown.

The idea that her dreams could hold such power and significance was both awe-inspiring and terrifying. Something about this specific nightmare made it stand out, something that demanded her attention.

Nick walked into the room holding a steaming cup of coffee. Soft morning light filtered through the curtains and cast a gentle glow across the bed. With a gentle smile, he drew closer, his eyes reflecting profound love and tenderness.

"Good morning! Here's your coffee," Nick said warmly, extending the cup towards Elira. His love for her radiated in every gesture, and he enjoyed these moments when he could pamper her with simple acts of kindness. Sometimes, he brewed coffee just to rouse her from her slumber, savoring the sleepy smile that always graced her lips.

"Good morning, thank you," she replied, her eyes meeting his with intense emotions. "I saw my mom's funeral in my dream last night. I wanted to..." continued Elira calmly. But before she could finish, Nick interrupted her gently.

"I'm running late, love. I really have to go!" he said, kissing her. His way of leaving always brought a smile to her face. He avoided morning conversations, understanding that her dreams tended to be unsettling.

As Nick walked towards the door, Elira remained seated, sipping her coffee while her mind drifted back to her dream. The vision had been haunting, leaving her feeling vulnerable and uncertain.

Sighing, she set the cup aside and went to the kitchen. Once there, she carefully toasted two slices of bread until they were perfectly golden brown. She then spread a generous layer of honey over both slices. This simple act had become her ritual and provided her comfort when times were difficult. Toasted bread with honey had always been her favorite, bringing her back to good days. She could forgo any meal, but not this one. It held a taste of nostalgia, warmth, and love that was irreplaceable.

After breakfast, Elira couldn't shake the lingering feeling that her unsettling dream needed attention. She picked up her mobile, dialed Teo's number, and set up a meeting for shopping and lunch. She knew Teo would be there to listen and support her; she always was.

Teo's presence alone was a soothing balm to Elira's unease. They had an unspoken understanding that allowed them to share their fears and secrets.

Their steps synchronized in harmony as they wandered through the mall's stores. Elira finally gathered the courage to broach the subject haunting her. Taking a deep breath, she turned to Teo, her eyes searching for alleviation in the depths of her friend's gaze.

"Teo, I had the strangest nightmare ever last night." There was a vulnerability in Elira's tone, a need to undergo the weight of her troubling dream with the one person she trusted most in the world.

"Again?" answered Teo excitedly.

"This was really bad, a horrible, horrible nightmare," Elira admitted, her voice heavy with the memory of her distressing dream. "You were in my dream, too, Teo. Should I be worried?"

"Oh, I'm okay, don't worry about me. Tell me about your dream."

Teo's curiosity was piqued, as it always was when Elira shared her dreams. She had long been envious of her friend's ability to remember her dreams when she couldn't recall one. But this time, something was different.

As Elira's words painted the terrible picture of her dream, Teo froze. The impact of the dream's content settled in, sending shivers down her spine.

Their shared interest in philosophy, the mysteries of the afterlife, and the unknown had often led them to ponder the unanswerable questions of existence. But now, it seemed their intellectual curiosity had taken a haunting turn.

"Call your mom," Teo urged, her concern overriding her fascination with premonitions.

Elira's hands trembled as she dialed the number, and her heart pounded with fear as she waited for her mother to answer. After agonizing moments, she hung up and continued with a quivering voice, "It was my dad. He asked me to come home. My mother is bedridden." After a short silence, she continued, "I'm going home today!"

Teo grew increasingly concerned. "I'll go with you," she vowed, determined to support her friend during this uncertain time.

"My dad told me that she is refusing to go to the hospital," said Elira. "He mentioned something about a flu epidemic, and the doctor suggested that it would be better to wait. I don't know what to think."

Teo couldn't help but reflect on the sinister connection between the dream and the real world unfolding before them. It was a surreal moment, a convergence of dreams and reality that neither of them had anticipated, and it left Teo with a sense of foreboding that hung heavy in the air.

Elira's appetite had vanished, and her fork pushed around the untouched steak on her plate. Her mind was elsewhere.

In the stifling atmosphere, she discreetly texted Nick, her fingers trembling as she composed the message. She needed to let him know that she would be visiting her parents for several days, though she couldn't explain the full extent of her emotions.

"Let me come with you. Don't go alone." Teo said again, almost crying.

"No Teo! You know my mom. I'd better go alone. I'll call you if I need you."

Everyone knew that Liv was less comfortable with guests. Falling ill at a young age, she erected a barrier between herself and others. Her home became a private refuge where she could freely grapple with her pain.

With a quick goodbye to Teo, Elira rose from the table and left, her footsteps echoing the unspoken fears that had driven her away.

Consumed by a gnawing dread, Teo couldn't shake the haunting feeling that she might never see Elira's mother again. As her thoughts whirled like a storm, she whispered, "Elira likes to think that there is always hope." It was a frail lifeline to cling to, a glimmer of optimism in the darkness. Worried, she reached for her phone and dialed Nick's.

The truth was an elusive and painful thing to accept. Elira struggled with the inevitable reality that everything, including life itself, had to end at some point. Her mother's illness had thrust her into a disorienting dance between worlds, where she often saw her mom teetering on the edge of the eternal, only to return to the confines of the mortal land. Hope and despair, a relentless tug-of-war between life and death that Elira could neither fully embrace nor face head-on.

Elira had already endured the heart-wrenching pain of losing someone special. When her beloved grandmother passed away, she felt lost. But soon after, she found peace in the comforting embrace of faith and the mysterious power of the divine.

She sought refuge from the unrelenting storm of grief and turned to the old church she used to frequent. Alone in the hallowed halls, she knelt before the worn pews, closed her eyes, and prayed.

Elira's gaze then rose to the magnificent fresco that adorned the church's ceiling. A tale of faith and friendship. In that sacred moment, she felt a connection to ages past, as if centuries of human suffering and resilience had pressed upon her shoulders. She stared at Isaac, silently thanking him for being a friend even in the face of unimaginable challenges.

The recollection of that day held a special place in Elira's heart. It served as a powerful example of the healing power of faith and the strength that could be found in the bonds of friendship, even in the darkest times.

As she confronted the uncertain future of her mother's illness, she held to the memory of that church, that fresco, and the belief that somewhere, somehow, there would be a way to find relief.

V

If only it could be a lucid dream and not a profound nightmare. Elira wanted a dream in which she was conscious of what she was dreaming. She had read about lucid dreamers who can influence their vision by changing the whole dream story's action. That would be too easy, too easy for her!

Dreams are believed to reflect the most personal thoughts, feelings, fears, and desires. Elira had internalized this theory for as long as she could remember. As evidence, she had the renowned psychologist Freud, who believed dreams are windows into our subconscious and allow us to satisfy urges that society deems unacceptable. Elira was fascinated by his work; while studying him in her psychology classes, she almost felt sorry that a teacher like him doesn't exist nowadays.

During the dead of night, when reality seemed distant, she often found herself dreaming of solutions and paths forward in situations where, in waking life, she felt lost and uncertain. As strange as they appeared, her dreams, if not nightmares, always provided answers.

Elira's grandmother told her that in Ancient Egypt, dreams were seen as divine messages, while in the Holy Bible, they were believed to foretell the future. This knowledge had lived inside her since she was a little girl, long before she fully understood its significance.

Elira later discovered that her grandmother's teachings were deeply rooted in Ancient Egyptian beliefs. In this tradition, dreaming of dogs signaled the presence of an enemy, while the sight of blood foretold shame. Yet, the most poignant lesson Elira absorbed was that dreaming of Death—whether her own or someone else's—meant that Death had passed by, leaving that person destined for a long life.

Coincidences, superstitions, premonitions, dreams—where was the truth and its meaning? Elira never stopped digging into this mystery. She relied on her instinct, and where instinct took her over the limit of normal and close to madness, as described by those who do not believe in anything, she consulted with Teo. Together, they were an indescribable intellectual and spiritual force.

One night, Elira had dreamed of an unfamiliar place beneath a mysterious bridge where the sun shone unnaturally. A strange vision unfolded before her eyes as she strolled along the cobblestone path—coins scattered across the asphalt, totaling 2.60 euros. It was an ordinary dream, but what followed left her questioning reality and fantasy.

Elira chose to walk to work the morning after her dream. It was a lovely day and a chance to exercise. As her feet carried her forward, a glint of something shiny on the ground caught her eye. It was a two-euro coin, and she picked it up. With the following four steps, she found four more coins! Step and twenty cent coin, step and twenty cent coin, step and ten cent coin, step and ten cent coin. Ultimately, the sum amounted to 2.60 euros, mirroring the exact amount from her dream.

Elira couldn't explain it then, and she couldn't explain it now. The mysterious occurrence remained an enigma, an unsettling problem that defied the boundaries of science and reason.

Would the experts also dismiss this as a simple coincidence in their quest for rationality? Or would they, too, be left baffled by the inexplicable connection between a dream and the waking world?

The inexplicable sequence of events that defined Elira's dream had left her bewildered and shocked. She had retraced her steps, double-checked her surroundings, and examined the coins meticulously, searching for any rational explanation that might ease her mind. But none was to be found. She remembered reading an article about precognitive dreams, where one experiences visions during sleep that may predict the future, suggesting that consciousness may be a part of reality. It was a confusing and paranormal phenomenon.

When she confided in Teo about the aforementioned hypnagogic experience, her friend could only offer a sympathetic smile. "A gift or a curse," Teo mused, echoing the thoughts swirling in Elira's mind. The line between these two possibilities blurred, and Elira was left to grapple with the profound implications of a dream manifesting so vividly in reality.

For Elira, it was a gift in that her dreams had transcended the limits of the subconscious, becoming a tangible force in her life. It was also a curse, leaving her with the unsettling realization that the world held mysteries far beyond the grasp of science.

The incident changed their perception of dreams,

pushing the limits of knowledge and questioning the idea that everything could easily be a coincidence. It was a reminder that the universe was vast and enigmatic, and sometimes, it revealed its secrets in ways that defied comprehension.

Elira and Teo were deep in thought as they pondered the mysterious connection between their dreams and reality. They couldn't help but wonder if their dreams held more secrets than they ever imagined. Looking into the unknown was driven by a hunger for answers that would change their perception of the line separating the world of wakefulness and the domain of dreams.

VI

The doctors were having a hard time because of the flu epidemic, not with the patients but with their relatives. Of course, the new flu epidemic was not as bad as the media said, but still scary.

People feared the political game, the restrictions, and how they introduced death. They also feared being unable to help because orders tied hands. Besides hope, the only option is to find a good doctor who sees a human being in a patient and not a money machine, a doctor with a heart who cares. Unfortunately, this is an endangered species.

In the medical community, the relationship between doctors and patients had turned into a covert operation that followed a set of unspoken and illegal rules. In the quiet hallways, a dubious agreement between the doctor and the patient, which determined the level of care provided, was made in hushed tones. An envelope was passed from one hand to another, carrying the implicit agreement.

This secret exchange was rooted in financial offerings, a crude measure of the level of care one could expect. The more money one was willing to part with, the deeper the bond of trust and, theoretically, the more attention one could secure from the doctor.

Sadly, those who couldn't afford to participate found themselves consigned to fate or a higher power for salvation. The doctors operated in the shadows of privilege, where wealth determined who received a chance at life and who became another statistic in the cold records of mortality. Families with empty pockets faced the bitter truth of a merciless system where the price of a loved one's survival was set by those in medical authority.

There were no guarantees, even with an envelope, but it was a desperate act of hope, a last-ditch effort to ensure the best care.

As if the heart-wrenching ordeal of battling illness weren't enough, a sinister underbelly tainted the world of medicine — the shadows where killer doctors lurked. These brilliant surgeons, betraying their sacred oath, traded lives for money, preying on the vulnerability of desperate families. In the murky depths, they operated with deadly precision, promising miraculous success in the most intricate and challenging surgeries, often targeting elderly patients grappling with terminal illnesses.

The particular assurances, fueled by the desperate yearning to prolong the lives of loved ones, were nothing but a dreadful illusion. In their pursuit of enormous paychecks, these unscrupulous healers turned executioners exploited the trust bestowed upon them. They whispered promises that veiled invitations to a deadly game, an illusion that crumbled in the face of cold, hard reality.

Liv's first surgical intervention took place in a public hospital. She needed a double bypass, a procedure that could save her life, a life already hanging by a fragile thread.

Among the patients, an old woman's plight echoed the bleakness of the situation. Her life balanced precariously on the precipice of mortality. The cruel twist of fate was that she had medical insurance, yet the doctor had postponed the surgery. Her chances of survival were determined not solely by her medical condition but by the size of the envelope gift demanded by the doctor.

The envelope's contents held the power to determine life or death, a chilling testament to the depths of despair and moral decay within the medical world.

The old woman's options dwindled until her desperation reached its zenith—the only solution lay in relinquishing her house, a symbolic gesture of surrender to the whims of destiny.

In this sea of misfortune, hope emerged from Elira's father, a man of compassion and selflessness. He took a loan, investing in saving a life. Buying her house would allow her to live the remaining days in comfort and peace in her own home. It was a race against time, a frantic battle against the relentless march of the end.

Unfortunately, death emerged victorious, claiming the fragile heart that could no longer withstand the burdens imposed by a callous system. It was a sad reminder that despite acts of kindness, the force of mortality often had the final say, leaving behind sadness and unfulfilled hopes.

Doctor Paula, a rare exemplar of honesty and integrity, strongly advised Elira's mother to remain home until the flu epidemic abated. She stood alone as a paragon of virtue in a medical world tainted by corruption. In stark contrast to her peers, she rejected the tainted envelope and accepted only yellow roses, symbols of hope and healing, but only once her patients emerged from danger.

Religion was the bedrock of her moral compass, a deep-seated faith in God that resonated with Elira's mother. Despite their long doctor-patient relationship, their interactions remained strictly professional, devoid of genuine friendship. While Doctor Paula's kindness was palpable, it was incongruent with her aversion to severely ill patients, a sentiment that simmered beneath her controlled exterior.

Even with her impeccable record—free of medical errors, abuse, or complaints—a mysterious antipathy had taken root within her, a restrained and enigmatic emotion that tainted her interactions.

This time, Elira had made an unshakeable decision. She could no longer stand idly by, witnessing her mother's health deteriorate further, nor could she endure the haunting nightmares that plagued her sleep. Driven by urgency and a foreboding sense of dread, she resolved to take matters into her own hands, heedless of permissions or counsel.

The unusual circumstances surrounding her mother, along with the constant premonitions that disturbed her nights, drove her to take action. She was ready to find a way through the troubles ahead.

With resolute self-confidence, Elira's thoughts echoed like a solemn vow. "This time, I won't listen; they will!" she silently affirmed, almost trying to convince herself first.

The weight of responsibility rested squarely on her shoulders, and she was prepared to forge her own path, disregarding convention and the advice of others. The nightmares that troubled Elira's nights became a relentless call to action, a summons she could no longer ignore.

Even if her mom would not be happy with her choice, even if it meant challenging the medical establishment, she knew she had to win this fight. Determination, love, and faith were her weapons.

VII

Liv's room was cloaked in shadows, and a dense, oppressive odor hung in the air, a haunting reminder of the suffering that had taken root within those walls. As Elira entered, her heart sank at the sight that greeted her. Her mother lay still, immersed in the pallor of illness, lost in fitful sleep. The pain was obvious.

Elira approached her mother with a hushed reverence, her voice a gentle whisper as she spoke,"Mom, how are you? Mom?" She yearned for a flicker of hope in her mother's response, a sign that the darkness might one day fade away.

"She just calmed down. She just fell asleep." Elira's dad paused, very sad. He continued, "Come, my child, let's go to the kitchen to talk. I'll make you something to eat."

"Tell me the truth, how is she really doing?"

"It's bad. Since yesterday, your mother can't get out of bed. A lot of pain, my child, she's in a lot of pain."

"What did Doctor Paula say? Did Mom call her, or did she lie again?"

"She told me she did. I don't know. You know your mother."

Liv had always maintained secrecy around her interactions with Doctor Paula, a veil of mystery that she draped over their medical consultations. From the outset of her illness, she had been unshakable in her instructions to her family.

"I will tell you everything you must know about my

health," she once said, her voice determined. "If you have anything to ask, ask me, not Doctor Paula."

It was a protective gesture of love and a fierce desire to shield her child and husband from the facts. She believed that by keeping them uninformed, they could live their lives unburdened by the constant shadow of illness.

Taking charge of her health and managing consultations and medical decisions was an act of empowerment for Liv. It was a means to an end—a strong declaration of her will to survive without disturbing anyone she held dear.

Within the complex loop of her disease, Elira's mother's purpose shone brilliantly—to live and protect her family, even if it meant veiling her struggles in a shroud of enigmatic isolation.

"Go have some rest, Dad. I'll watch Mom now," Elira said.

"In a while, darling. I'll keep you company until I get tired," he answered.

"As you wish, Dad. As you wish."

"Let's go to your mother's room. Let's keep an eye on her," he said, walking out of the kitchen.

Elira observed her father, his weariness etched deeply into his features. Fatigue had settled upon him, and sadness clouded his eyes. It had been a trying period, with sleep eluding him for over two long days. What had happened with his wife bore down on his shoulders.

In the soft quiet of the room, they both maintained a vigil at Elira's mother's bedside, yearning for the moment when she would stir from her slumber. It was late, and exhaustion clung to her father like a relentless adversary. He could finally entertain the notion of a brief respite—a short nap that might offer a modicum of support.

As her parents succumbed to the solace of sleep, Elira seized a moment of opportunity. She carefully retrieved her mother's cell phone, her heart pounding with anticipation. Her fingers trembled slightly as she began to scroll through the messages between her mother and Doctor Paula, determined to uncover the hidden secrets within those digital exchanges.

Words and phrases leaped off the screen, each carrying its gravity in the cryptic dialogue that unfolded before Elira's eyes. "Pain," "afraid," "my child," "help," "please," "dying," "stay home," "it's not safe," "you'll die," "hospital," "emergency," "hope," "can't." These fragmented messages panicked Elira.

The truth became undeniable as Elira pieced together the fragments of conversation. Doctor Paula had indeed advised Liv to stay at home to endure the unrelenting pain for as long as she could bear it. Going to the hospital during the flu epidemic was risky, a gamble with life itself. The question echoed ominously in Elira's mind: how can one endure such pain?

As Elira stared at the messages that had shattered the illusion of trust, a storm of questions raged within her. Why had a doctor advised her critically ill mother to remain within the confines of their home? Did the hospital not possess measures to shield its vulnerable patients from the merciless grasp of the threat? And perhaps the most haunting inquiry of all: how much anguish should a person endure before a doctor deems it necessary to intervene and offer the mercy of hospitalization.

For the first time, Elira was on the brink of confronting Doctor Paula. Whether welcomed or not, Elira's voice was about to be heard—filled with questions, ready to put an end to her mother's suffering.

"You're awake!" Elira's voice filled with joy as she beheld her mother sitting in bed.

"Mom, how do you feel?" Elira inquired anxiously, "Are you in pain? Do you need anything?" Her words tumbled out, a cascade of worry and affection, as she eagerly awaited her mother's response, hoping that this marked the beginning of brighter days ahead.

"Yes, but don't worry. I'll take a pill, and it will go away," Liv reassured, summoning a faint smile that masked her discomfort.

"Mom?!" Elira's voice quivered with concern, her brows furrowing in worry.

"Hm..."

"I think we should call Doctor Paula."

"No! End of the conversation!" Her mother's swift response left no room for further discussion.

"Okay. What about calling an ambulance? She must come if we call the ambulance. Please!" Elira's plea held an urgency born of concern as she sought any means to ensure her mother received the care she needed.

Liv suddenly fell asleep again, seemingly exhausted by the effort of the conversation.

The room, shrouded in dappled morning light, desperately needed change. Old curtains, timeworn furniture, and faded wallpaper contributed to a sense of despair within those walls.

Elira felt that a change was necessary, not only in the room's design but also in their lives. Her mother had been reluctant to redecorate, holding onto what was familiar and comfortable. It was daunting, but Elira would take it on if it meant bringing happiness and optimism back into their home.

"Ca... call ambu... call your father. Ambul... Air." Liv's voice trembled with each sound, a laborious effort as she fought to breathe. In the blink of an eye, her pallor turned a ghastly shade of blue.

Panic seized the room while Elira, with fear, grabbed the phone to dial for an ambulance. Her father, no stranger to the terror that gripped them, was already by Liv's side, desperately trying to aid her faltering breath.

"Air, outside...my chil...I can't brea..." She struggled to pronounce the word; every inhale felt like a precious moment slipping away.

The wailing siren of the ambulance pierced the air as it arrived within an astonishing ten minutes. Elira stood there, tears streaming down her face as she begged the paramedics to save her mother.

While the medical team rushed to attend to her mother, Elira couldn't help but think about the envelope procedure, a practice she had heard whispers of but had never dared to use herself. She knew that without it, they might not save her mother. With trembling hands, she turned to her father, the urgency in her voice cutting through her fear.

"How much should we pay them?" she implored, the question laced with anxiety. But her father, upset by the image before his eyes, couldn't muster a response. His fear had rendered him speechless, leaving Elira alone thinking about the uncertainty.

"Please, doctor, please save my mom." Elira said with raw desperation as she handed over the money, more than the usual cost, an offering to transform the indifference of the ambulance staff into a quick effort to save Liv's life. At that moment, the price was irrelevant; all that mattered was securing the medical care her mother needed.

Grateful, the medical team immediately sprang into action and also efficiently provided Elira with a sedative to ease her suffering. But Elira declined, choosing to bear the crushing weight of her heartbreak and the swelling pain in her eyes.

A nurse gently positioned an oxygen mask over Elira's mother's mouth as the doctor closely watched her blood pressure. Another nurse administered medication, and finally, her mother's breathing resumed. It marked a small victory, a delicate moment of relief in their challenging ordeal.

Nonetheless, their path was still far from its end. The hospital lay ahead, and they would continue the battle to save Liv's life. *Or not!*

Even if Liv was used to hospitalization, this time was different. Due to the restrictions, it was a challenging moment, maybe the hardest ever. Now, Liv will be totally alone. No one, absolutely no one, will be able to be by her side in the hospital.

But Liv will not cave! Neither Elira! How could they when life itself showed them that miracles happen? How could Liv give up on fighting for her life with a cruel illness when, by statistics and medical research, she should be already dead? How could Elira give up when she saw her mom as a winner? Liv always wins!

VIII

Nightmares had become one with reality. Reality had become a horror. Every life had an end. Elira knew it, yet she couldn't handle her mother's end. She wondered if a dream could be real life and the tragedy she was living be a dream, and the choice of this version of life is because her mom was still alive, not dead like in the last nightmare.

A car stopped in front of the house, distracting Elira from the bizarre thoughts. Teo and Nick arrived unexpectedly, bringing a flicker of joy. Their presence was invaluable, especially for Elira's father. He can now return to his daily routine, gardening, cooking, and doing everything possible to avoid sadness. He promised that to his wife. He promised it since Elira was a baby, never knowing when illness would become death. He never learned how to behave with his daughter; he was always afraid not to say something wrong and make her downcast more than she was.

"Bless those kids," he murmured, heading to the garden.

While Elira's father was gardening, all the rest were hanging in the living room, waiting for a phone call from the hospital. Several hours had passed since the ambulance left, yet there was no news.

"Why don't you call Dr. Paula?" asked Teo, breaking the

silence.

"I already did, many times. She doesn't answer. Damn it!" answered Elira nervously.

"It's Saturday. Maybe she's not working," said Nick, trying to calm Elira.

"I don't care. She is online on WhatsApp. I also texted her to explain the situation. She ignores me." Elira was getting more nervous.

The ambulance doctor instructed Elira to await a call from the hospital, which left her feeling powerless and mired in a painful state of uncertainty. In such moments, the virtue of patience could transform into a form of torment as time seemed to stretch endlessly before her.

The persistent reporting of the flu epidemic had complicated matters, making it challenging to find anyone willing to accept a bribe for access to the hospital's inner sanctum.

It was inconceivable that the excuse of a Saturday or the prevailing epidemic should deter Dr. Paula from responding to the urgent call. Undoubtedly, the hospital had alerted her to the danger that had befallen Elira's mother, casting a lot of responsibility upon her shoulders.

The minutes ticked by, each laden with a sense of impending reckoning as Elira grappled with the unsettling truth that her mother's life hung precariously in the balance, and the waiting game had become an agonizing test of endurance.

Like the rest of the house, the living room needed changes. The old furniture, the dusty books, and the little antique souvenirs thrown here and there had a negative impact. Redecoration was the only viable remedy at this juncture, and a thought occurred to Elira.

"As soon as we receive any news from the hospital, we should consider redecorating the entire house," she declared optimistically. "It might bring some joy to my mom and infuse the house with new energy. What if the darkness of all this old stuff is affecting her? What if it's holding her back?" continued Elira, prompting a puzzled exchange of glances between Teo and Nick, who regarded her with concern and disbelief.

"Honey, I don't think your parents will agree to that," Nick gently cautioned, his tone filled with understanding. "The things in this house, whether old or new, hold their memories. It's a part of who they are."

Nick's sentiment was mirrored by Teo, who nodded in agreement. "He's right. Right now, we need to focus on Liv's health. Let's try to call the hospital. The emergency room's number should be available online. There's no other place they would have taken her."

After countless attempts to reach the emergency room, someone finally picked up the phone, shattering the oppressive silence of the late-night hours. Midnight had gone, and they would eventually get the answers they desperately sought. However, what they encountered was nothing short of apocalyptic.

A young female voice, eerily calm and almost cruel in its composure, identified herself as a doctor on the other end of the line. In a tone that sent chills down Elira's spine, she revealed that her mother had contracted the new flu, a simple statement that seemed incongruous with the severity of the problem. Because of this merciless viral assailant, her mother struggled to breathe, and the medical team had been forced to resort to intubation.

The news landed like a thunderbolt, shattering Elira's world. She was left in stunned disbelief, unable to reconcile this grim reality with the fact that her mother had been at home just hours ago, and no one in their family had exhibited any signs of the flu. It was absolutely impossible, a terrific revelation that sent tremors of despair and disbelief coursing through her veins.

It had been a lost battle for Elira, contesting the doctor's assertion. Her mother couldn't have been infected as nobody close to her ever was. And she had never left the house since the epidemic started. But the doctor's response, delivered with a chilling blend of cruelty, coldness, and creepy calmness, rendered Elira speechless.

"Oh, I know, I know. She got infected here, from us, in the hospital. I will keep you updated," were the last words the young doctor imparted before severing the connection. Like sharp-edged blades, those words carved themselves deep into Elira's consciousness, leaving an indelible mark that would linger as a haunting specter for the entirety of her life. The world had shifted irrevocably. Guilt and despair descended upon her shoulders, leaving her powerless in the face of woe that had unfolded beyond her control.

A dense fog invaded Elira's mind, accompanied by waves of nausea and an overwhelming sense of shock. She could hear the faint murmur of Teo and Nick engaged in conversation, but her ability to react had been swallowed by the strong tide of emotions.

Her father was already sleeping, undisturbed by the concerns that had beset their hearts. There was no rush to burden him with the unsettling news just yet. Better in the morning, clinging to the hope that the night would pass without any further misfortune.

The prospect of survival was hanging by a thread for her mother, tormented by a heart condition and many ailments. In this dark and uncertain hour, the only light of optimism emanated from the divine as Elira held to the belief that preserving her mother's fragile existence would take nothing short of a miracle.

"Dr. Paula was right," Elira finally said. "She knew this would happen. She told my mom not to go to the hospital."

"No, no. It's not like that." Nick said.

"Right, she would probably be dead if you hadn't called the ambulance," added Teo.

"Perhaps you are both right," Elira said. "How am I supposed to live without my mom? I don't want her to die." And she threw herself into Nick's arms, crying.

Whatever they said would have been unhelpful. There were no words for such a sadness. Nothing could ease the hell of anticipating a loved one's death, either the heartache that followed. Only time offered any hope, though it was a fickle ally—sometimes it healed, and other times it drove one to madness.

Elira was acutely aware of her own vulnerability despite her extensive knowledge and experience with emotional expectations. She was well-versed in interpreting dreams and comforting those facing desperate circumstances. Yet, life's cruelties often defied reason and compassion. The advice she readily gave to others was a bitter pill for her to swallow herself. In her struggle, she needed a distraction—perhaps redecorating the house would provide a temporary escape from the cruel ache.

IX

During their college years, Elira and Teo found joy in academics and the thrilling blend of fun. On weekends, the local club was a refuge from life's challenges.

In the pulsing rhythm of the club, Elira and Teo discovered a unique kind of mastery—the power of control that shielded them from the alluring whispers of harmful temptations. Dancing provided a refuge where concerns dissolved, respecting limits and declining detrimental choices.

Elira and Teo stood firm amidst the societal landscape of experimentation in college, where many tended to surrender control. Despite the universal allure of drugs and the haze of intoxication that enveloped their generation, they never gave in. They chose to carve a different narrative, which served as a witness to revelry without succumbing to the delicate unknowns lurking in the shadows of their collegiate experience.

Elira stepped into the nightclub, her flowing blonde hair cascading down her shoulders like a golden waterfall. She radiated confidence and grace. Her eyes shimmered with a magic spark, and her smile exuded a hypnotic charm that drew people's attention. Known among her friends for her beauty and kindness, she was indeed a unique individual.

On the other side of the crowded club stood Nick, a man of captivating intelligence and handsome features who turned heads wherever he went. Dressed in a tailored suit accentuating his muscular physique, he looked fearless. His blue eyes held a spark of curiosity and a hint of mystery.

Without words, they sensed an inexplicable connection —a magnetic pull that drew them closer together. Fate intervened! Elira and Nick's paths crossed as they reached for a drink at the bar, their eyes locking for a brief moment that felt like an eternity.

Nick struck up a conversation with a confident grin, his intelligence and wit immediately captivating Elira's attention. They found themselves effortlessly engaged in a lively discussion about topics ranging from art and culture to their dreams and aspirations. It was as if their minds were in perfect resonance, each thought flowing seamlessly into the next.

Elira, usually cautious, felt unexpected comfort around Nick. His genuine interest in her opinions and his ability to make her laugh dispelled any nervousness she might have had. Nick, in turn, was drawn to Elira's beauty, kindness, and elegance.

As the night continued, they moved to the dance floor, bodies swaying to the rhythm of the music. Their chemistry was strong, the electricity between them almost tangible. The world around them faded into the background as they lost themselves in each other's company, sharing stories and dreams, laughter and whispers.

When the night drew to a close, Nick and Elira found themselves outside, the fantastic night air a stark contrast to the heat of the dance floor. They stood facing each other until Nick stepped closer, his hand gently brushing against

Elira's cheek.

"I feel like we've known each other forever," Nick whispered, his eyes fixed on hers.

Elira smiled, her heart racing. "Me too."

And at that moment, beneath the moonlit sky, Elira and Nick sealed their connection with a kiss. That kiss promised a future filled with shared adventures, laughter, and the undeniable certainty that they were a perfect match, brought together by fate.

After much contemplation, they reached a mutual decision: marriage was not the path meant for them. Their love was strong, yet they found that the traditional institution of marriage didn't align with their ideals. They shared a life brimming with happiness, choosing to cherish each moment without the need for formal vows. Hand in hand, they walked a unique journey, finding fulfillment in their own way, unburdened by societal expectations. Their choice was evidence of the beauty of forging a relationship on their terms, a life filled with joy as they continued to build a future together, side by side.

Nick's remarkable capacity to stand persistently beside his beloved girlfriend during a challenging juncture, marked by her sadness and heartfelt concern for her mother's well-being, epitomized a gesture of genuine love and his inherent qualities as a virtuous person.

X

It was late at night, and Nick was worried after trying to reach Elira over the cell phone many times. He texted, called, and tried to locate her via GPS tracking, but nothing. She had just vanished.

The previous night, the group had retired early, but a jarring awakening for water revealed Elira's absence.

Even Teo was at a loss regarding her sudden disappearance. The weight of Elira's distress over her mother's hospitalization lingered in Nick's mind; the circumstances were undoubtedly emotionally taxing. The epidemic's stringent restrictions had already taken a toll on Elira's spirits, amplified by her inability to be by her mother's side or engage in face-to-face discussions with the doctors.

"Don't worry. She's probably taking a walk. She'll be back," Teo said to comfort Nick.

"Are you kidding me? In the middle of the night," answered nervous Nick. "I'm going to wake up her father."

"No, let him sleep, poor man. He's going through a lot already. Stop being worried. She will come back. She probably had a nightmare again."

"Okay," said Nick, continuing, "But I'm going to look for her around the neighborhood."

"Nick, please, don't. Give her some space. That's why she didn't want us to come here in the first place," insisted Teo.

He knew that Teo was right, better than anybody else. His love for Elira was so big that it was tough to wait, even though Nick was always rational and calm.

With the first rays of sunrise, Nick felt a sense of relief as Elira reappeared. The tension that gripped him was finally released.

In the quiet aftermath, no words were exchanged. A collective decision was made to stand by Elira, giving her a supportive presence. The unspoken consensus prevailed, a testament to their compassion and friendship. No inquiries were made about the ordeal Elira had put Nick through, as he recognized the depth of her emotional turmoil and chose empathy over curiosity. It was a subtle yet profound demonstration of their unity and understanding, reassuring Elira that she was not alone in her struggle.

"I'm sorry, Nick," Elira said.

In the coming days, Elira, Nick, and Teo diligently transformed the house. The rooms underwent a remarkable metamorphosis, reflecting the trio's creativity and shared vision for a revitalized living space.

Elira guided the redecoration process; she led Nick and Teo in carefully moving furniture, selecting fresh colors, and hanging captivating artworks that breathed new life into the surroundings. The walls, once adorned with fading memories, now bore vibrant shades that injected energy into every corner.

As a perfect team, they organized all the old stuff into boxes so Elira's mom would not be upset when she returned from the hospital. In fact, the changes made to the house could only make her happy.

Elira's father observed the bustling activity with a

contented smile. He was pleased to see his daughter in a good mood again. The sound of hammers and chatter echoed through the halls, serving as a comforting reminder that life was moving forward, even in hard times.

However, the project's backdrop was shaded with a bad feeling. Elira's mother showed no improvement as time passed. Dr. Paula's prognosis had cast a shadow of despair, indicating that Liv's condition was too critical to yield the desired results. The uncertainty contrasted sharply with the activity within the home.

As the redecoration continued, they oscillated between hope and heartache. The vibrant colors and renewed aesthetics were proof of their strength, a tangible reminder that life persisted in adversity. While Elira's mother's health remained precarious, they found consolation in the transformation around them, symbolizing their intense spirit and persistence in creating beauty despite life's challenges.

Once finished, the rooms looked like they were cut out of interior design magazines, reflecting the effort and dedication to the project. Yet, as the days passed, the initial spark of hope ignited by the renovation began to wane.

The echoes of their laughter from the last few days seemed distant, a sign of the moments when the burden of reality had momentarily lifted.

Elira's conversations with Dr. Paula had become a routine. Every day, she would engage in these discussions, seeking updates on her mother's health and hoping for positive news. Despite her polite demeanor, Elira noticed an underlying tension in the doctor's voice.

While maintaining professionalism, Dr. Paula couldn't

hide the truth; the intubation had not led to the recovery they had desperately hoped for.

The strained nature of their chat mirrored the complex emotions at play. Elira grappled with a mixture of frustration, sadness, and the lingering hope that seemed to waver but never fully extinguish. On the other end of the line, Dr. Paula was tasked with delivering news that she knew Elira didn't want to hear.

XI

Days passed in a torturous procession, with Liv still trapped between life and death. Dr. Paula had adopted a starkly realistic tone, offering no false hope.

As they settled into this grim new normal, Teo received an unexpected message from her husband. She had been conspicuously absent from her own life, and this brief interlude had led her husband to a revelation. He had come to the scary idea that he could lose Teo to his demons, a harrowing prospect that filled him with dread.

Driven by fear, Teo's husband decided to enroll in a program designed specifically for his struggle, fully aware that having her by his side was necessary for their future.

"I have to go," Teo gently informed Elira. She looked at her friend with understanding, knowing that life demanded her presence elsewhere. "But remember, no matter what you need, just call me."

Elira nodded, her eyes reflecting gratitude. She couldn't help but feel happy about the positive turn of events. She had always wanted nothing but the best for Teo and her husband.

Amid the storm that had engulfed their lives, this good news was a promise, a reminder that even in the darkest times, there could still be moments of brightness.

Elira understood the immense courage it took to

acknowledge one's addiction and seek help, especially when it was as insidious as gambling. She knew the path to recovery would be difficult, but she also believed in the power of love and fearlessness to overcome even the most daunting obstacles.

"Don't worry, Teo. Go, he needs you more than I do." Elira said. "I have Nick. He's helping a lot. Go and save your marriage."

After hours of heartfelt conversations, during which Teo shared her happiness, the moment of goodbye finally arrived. Teo had to leave that day, but only after extracting a promise from Elira. She looked into her friend's eyes and asked her once again to promise to call if any changes occurred.

Elira nodded solemnly, fully aware of the seriousness of her promise. Teo's concern was evident in every word and gesture, and Elira treasured their friendship more than ever in these trying times.

"Drive safe," Nick urged as they prepared to part ways. "And please, call us once you arrive," he added.

With their hearts filled with care and affection, they watched Teo leave, hoping for the best and praying that their lives would soon see better days.

Nick was caught in a whirlwind of emotions as he observed the evolving dynamics within their close-knit circle. Initially, he had anticipated that Teo's departure would bring added challenges for Elira, considering Teo's unique support. However, prepared for the worst, he soon witnessed a subtle transformation in Elira's demeanor that surprised him.

Instead of being burdened by Teo's absence, Elira seemed to breathe easier, her spirit visibly lifted. It was as if her heartfelt prayers for Teo's happiness had been heard, and her dear friend went on a journey toward rediscovered love and contentment with her husband.

But it wasn't just Teo's departure that had sparked a change in Elira. Her interactions with Nick also underwent a significant transformation. She emitted kindness, tenderness, and sensuality, which Nick had longed for in their relationship. As they faced the turbulent days ahead, their love evolved and deepened in ways they had never expected, creating a strong, passionate chemistry between them again.

Nick marveled at their desire for each other, a desire he had never dared to hope for. They began to make love again, and in those intimate moments, he witnessed Elira living again. Their love story was taking an unexpected turn, rekindling the flames of passion.

While her father often kept himself busy gardening or retired to his room, there was no guarantee of privacy. Nick was a wise and perceptive man. He understood that his passion and intimacy with Elira might be temporary.

His decision to purchase an apartment near Elira's father's place had been his long-held plan, waiting for the right opportunity. A businessman usually cautions now had to act fast, protecting Elira from the ugly, dangerous monster called depression.

In the middle of their extreme happiness, luck smiled upon Nick with a good deal, and the apartment in the building next door became his property.

"Oh my God, what did you do?" Elira exclaimed in astonishment. Nick's thoughtfulness and dedication left her both moved and grateful.

"You know I was looking to buy an apartment here. I

just had to wait for a good offer," Nick replied warmly. "I grabbed the opportunity."

"Of course you did!"

"Elira, darling, I think it will be good for you not to sleep in your parents' house. Don't you agree?"

"I guess. I don't know, darling." Elira said. "All I know is that I love you."

Tears of joy shimmered in Elira's eyes as she hugged Nick tightly, feeling his love surge through her like an electric current. In that embrace, their souls fused, creating an otherworldly bond that left her breathless and awash in warmth.

Elira's father genuinely welcomed the news. He had always believed that a young couple should have their own place, and this decision aligned with his values.

The change in Elira's mental state didn't go unnoticed. She appeared more confident and composed, especially when discussing her mother's matters with the doctor. It was as if finding this balance in her personal life had positively impacted her ability to cope with the challenges they faced.

Impressed by Nick's considerate nature and affection, Elira resolved to savor life's small, beautiful occasions. She recognized the wisdom in Nick's words: her mother was still alive, and there was no need to mourn her before the time came. Instead, she could be present in the moment and find happiness where it existed. After all, her mother would undoubtedly want her to be happy, to enjoy life's beauty despite all difficulties.

With each passing day, the two lovers drew closer, their bond deepening as they walked the razor's edge between pleasure and misery. Together, they learned that love could endure even in the face of life's trials, and they were determined to cherish every precious second they had.

Elira was taken aback by her behavior and newfound desires. She recognized the need for moments of happiness and escape from the ever-present pain that seemed destined never to fade completely. She was a brilliant, intelligent woman who cared for her relationship with Nick. She had to!

She might have hesitated to express her deep-seated feelings, perhaps even feeling ashamed about them. But now, no more excuses were holding her back.

She was ready to explore the depths of her desires and to revel in the profound connection she shared with the man she loved. For them, the flames of passion burned brighter than ever, igniting their hearts and souls in a love story that defied the odds.

As they settled into their new apartment, everything seemed almost perfect. Elira's nightmares had inexplicably ceased since their move. The reasons behind this abrupt change remained a mystery. Could it be the power of love? Or perhaps the simple act of not sleeping in her parents' house had broken the cycle of her nightmares.

Her focus remained on her mother, who was still intubated under the care of Dr. Paula, who offered little hope for a recovery. The enigma of the nightmares was just another layer in the complex panorama of their lives.

Elira couldn't help but wonder about the perplexing boundary between dreams and reality. It was as if the universe was playing a surreal game, blurring the lines of existence. An alternate dimension! She found herself yearning for a simple yet profound reversal of fate.

She had a fervent wish: if only her mother could get

well. Then she would believe that she was living a dream, and the harsh, painful reality that had enveloped them would become the haunting nightmare of the past.

What if the concept of a perfect life was an illusion? A mirage that shimmered on the horizon, forever eluding her grasp. It was as if the universe had conspired to intertwine the threads of happiness and unhappiness, never allowing one to exist without the other.

There was an unmistakable feeling of harmony in her new home with Nick, overshadowed by the ominous presence of illness—a constant alert to how fragile life was and how unpredictable fate could be.

Elira couldn't escape the unsettling thought that the existence of perfect dreams was a myth. Maybe, in the essence of her being, she had to juggle between joy and sadness, affection and heartbreak. A cryptic dilemma continued to haunt her life. *Again!*

"Oh God, I miss Teo." She found herself murmuring.

Only Teo could clear up the complicated confusion of Elira's philosophical musings. Their connection ran deep; they had woven threads of contemplation and introspection, delving into the mysteries of life and existence. Folie à deux, but not quite! For a delusion to be shared by two people, there must be two people, yet Teo had never experienced what her best friend did. She only imagined it, imagined so hard that she thought she felt it. Teo had been Elira's confidante, her intellectual companion in pursuing answers to life's most twisted questions.

Elira's exceptional ability to separate her strange thoughts from her time with Nick showcased their power as a couple. She was lucky to have a partner who understood her complexities. Nick valued the depth of her mind and felt her soul's warmth.

Working from home gave him the flexibility to support Elira closely. He recognized the importance of their united strength in these challenging times and aimed to be a steadfast supporter of his girlfriend.

Despite their idyllic relationship, Elira continued to be consumed by her philosophical inquiries. The essence of existence intrigued her, acting like an unseen current flowing through the depths of her being.

Like clockwork, Elira made her way to her father's house daily. They would sit together, mainly discussing Liv and sharing hopes.

Elira's father was a man of few words, a trait that had remained consistent throughout their lives. He had always been a quiet and contemplative person, speaking only when necessary and preferring actions to words. His approach to life had been shaped by years of tending to his garden, where the language of nature had spoken to him more greatly than any conversation.

Their mealtimes were moments of respite. Elira and her father would sit down to eat, and the simplicity of the ritual was a comforting anchor in their stormy lives.

After these meals, he would often return to his beloved garden, where he would immerse himself in the soothing embrace of loneliness. His greenhouse was his sanctuary, where he could find solace and quiet reflection amidst the world's chaos. In those moments, tending to his plants and flowers, he found a sense of peace that eluded him elsewhere.

XII

On a regular Sunday morning, Elira consciously visited the quaint village church, which held memories and a mystical connection she had nurtured over the years.

Waking up that day, a strong attraction to the place so loved by her grandmother stirred within her, and she couldn't resist the urge to follow her instinct. Then she remembered her dream. A peculiar dream, one veiled in mystery.

In the nocturnal reverie, she found herself running through the labyrinthine corridors of an ancient castle, its secrets whispered by the flickering candlelight. As she fled, pursued by shadows that seemed eerily like hers, she stumbled upon the foreboding entrance to a long-forgotten graveyard, where time had etched its dark history into the weathered gravestones. She was not scared. The way out was there: a grave, the answer. The map to the grave was the owl that suddenly appeared from nowhere. The shadows vanished when she saw a big black marble grave without a name. A presence tried to pull her into the grave. Elira woke up.

When she stepped inside the church, a familiar sense of nostalgia surrounded her. The sacred place had been a source of comfort and wonder throughout her life, and she had formed a magical friendship with Isaac, the famous figure depicted in the magnificent fresco at the heart of the church.

Once Elira approached the altar, she felt Isaac's presence. His eyes, captured in the splendid artwork, seemed to come alive, conveying a timeless wisdom beyond paint and canvas. Isaac's eyes met hers, and it was as if they shared a secret language.

In that perfect moment, with Isaac's eyes watching over her, Elira felt a deep sense of peace and belonging. It was as if she had come home to a place where the limits between the ordinary and the extraordinary blurred, where her connection with the mystical figure surpassed the confines of the church's walls. She felt that, with all her being, Isaac would be her messenger and carry her heartfelt prayer to God.

After she visited the church, Elira returned to her father's house. There, she found Nick patiently waiting, the dining table set for their shared meal. Over lunch, as they savored their food, Elira recounted her visit to the church. The wonder always accompanying her tales of Isaac captivated Nick and her father. Each time she spoke of him, it was as if a touch of magic and the divine graced their presence.

Subsequently, Nick excused himself; the workload that had piled up over the week was waiting for him. Sunday would be dedicated to catching up on his projects.

On that particular day, there was an atmosphere of subtle anxiety in Elira's father's newly redecorated house. The usual tranquility was disturbed, and a sense of impending change hung heavy. Elira's father deviated from his customary routine. Instead of retreating to his garden, he invited Elira into the elegantly refurbished living room for what appeared to be an unusual conversation.

Now adorned with modern furnishings and bathed in the soft glow of contemporary lighting, the room took on a strange stillness as they settled in. The temporary silence pressed down on them, creating tension.

Elira's father's demeanor was thoughtful, his typically composed features etched with a hint of concern. The lines on his face appeared deeper as if reflecting the moment's importance.

As they began their conversation, the shadows in the room seemed to move too fast, casting unique and elongated shapes on the walls. The large windows, dressed with contemporary drapes that allowed a measured amount of fading daylight to filter through, further enhanced the place of uncertainty.

"Sometimes," he said with unusual gravity, "life takes unexpected turns, and we find ourselves standing at the crossroads, unsure of the path to take. Your mother's condition, it's... you know, Elira."

Elira looked at her father, her eyes reflecting both curiosity and concern. "I know, Dad, but we can't give up now. We'll get through this together."

"Life can be brutal," he said. "We like to think that there is always hope."

"What do you mean?"

"Everything has to die. Your mom will die. That's the truth," he paused for a second. "I'll die! Each and every one of us."

Elira felt like the ground had been pulled from beneath her. Her eyes welled up with tears, but she refused to let them fall. "Dad, how can you say that? You're supposed to believe in her recovery, in miracles."

Her father's eyes bore into hers, full of a strange mix of

sadness and determination. "I do believe in miracles, Elira, but sometimes the greatest miracle is granting someone we love the peace they deserve, even if it means letting them go."

His words echoed in her mind, and she felt a wave of despair wash over her. She had always believed in hope, in the possibility of miracles. But now, faced with her father's uncompromising realism, she couldn't deny the truth.

Eventually, tears streamed down her face as she contemplated the unthinkable. She thought about her mother, lying unconscious in the hospital, fighting a battle against a bad illness. Thinking of losing her, of saying goodbye forever, was almost too much to bear.

She knew her father was right. She had to prepare herself for the worst, for the inevitable. But how could she let go of the woman who had been her rock, her confidante, her source of strength for her entire life? How could she say goodbye to her mother, her best friend?

As she stood there, lost in her confusion, she couldn't help but feel that a piece of her was slipping away, leaving an emptiness that nothing could fill. Liv's fragile existence pressed down on her like an oppressive shroud, and there was no escape.

The ringing phone shattered the silence that had settled in the room. Elira and Nick exchanged glances, startled by the unexpected call so late on a Sunday night. Elira's heart raced as she picked up the receiver, afraid of what news awaited her on the other end of the line.

"Hello?" she answered, her voice shaking nervously.

"Elira, it's Dr. Paula," came the calm and composed voice on the other end.

Elira's heart sank. She braced herself for the worst,

fearing that her mother had died. But then, Dr. Paula continued, "I wanted to let you know that there has been a change in your mother's condition."

Elira's breath caught in her throat, and her eyes widened in disbelief. She exchanged a bewildered look with Nick, who listened to the conversation.

"Her vital signs have improved slightly," Dr. Paula explained. "It's a small improvement, but it's there. I want permission to wake her and proceed to heart surgery."

Elira struggled to find her voice when asked, "Is there a chance that she could recover?"

Dr. Paula's response was cautious but also optimistic. "It's too early to say for certain, Elira. Your mother is still critical, and we're doing everything possible. But we need the surgery. Otherwise..."

Elira took a moment to gather her thoughts, her mind swirling with a blend of emotions.

"Can you guarantee that the surgery will save her life?" Elira finally asked, her voice reflecting skepticism.

"The chances of your mother's survival, Elira, are less than 50%," Dr. Paula said with empathy. "But without surgery, the chances are zero," she continued.

"I know my mom is a fighter," Elira said confidently.

"I wouldn't argue with that, but still, there are no guarantees in medicine, Elira. Though her vitals are meandering downhill. At this point, everything is systematically shutting down. But I can assure you that we have a highly skilled surgical team and will do everything possible to give your mother the best chance of survival." Dr. Paula said, losing her patience.

"Thank you, Dr. Paula," Elira whispered, her voice filled with gratitude. "Thank you for letting me know. I'll call you back first thing tomorrow morning."

As she hung up the phone, she turned to Nick, silently watching her anguish, and smiled tremblingly through her tears. She recalled her father's words, emphasizing that surgery remained their only lifeline, the slender thread connecting them to the possibility of a miracle.

A unanimous decision had been forged in the face of all-encompassing uncertainty and the daunting odds. Liv, frail and intubated, waged an arduous battle for her very existence, one that would culminate in a perilous heart surgery.

Karma, the irony of faith, took away Liv's right to decide for herself. She managed to keep her family away from the cruel pain of medical compromise. Now, her life hangs on Elira's right choice!

Unyielding questions swirled within Elira's mind like a tempest. Could her mother's fragile heart endure this harrowing ordeal? Did she possess enough fortitude to face this last, desperate skirmish for life?

With quiet fear and a strong will, Elira braced herself for the unknown path ahead. The surgery stood as a fragile lifeline, a bold challenge to impossible obstacles, and the faint promise of a new beginning.

XIII

Dr. Paula arranged a meeting between Elira and the surgeon, Dr. Jack. As Elira sensed, the impending discourse would delve into essential matters. Instinctively, she suspected that the focal point of their discussion would be the money.

The meeting took place in a nearby coffee shop, where the aroma of freshly brewed coffee blended with the bittersweet undercurrents of life-altering decisions.

Tall and robust, Doctor Jack's physique exuded strength and endurance, weathered by time. Despite lacking conventional sex appeal, there was a distinct charm about him. He was known as a respected doctor, was confident, and knew how to speak.

Elira noticed his tendency to flirt but skillfully redirected the conversation to her mother's imminent surgery. It wasn't the first time she had faced similar situations, and she knew how to play this game very well.

Doctor Jack, fascinated by Elira and happy about the big envelope he got, unexpectedly chose honesty over indifference. He shared the hard truth about what would happen, whether sparked by a genuine interest in Elira or influenced by the unexpected bonus.

"My dear, I don't think your mom will survive. Her heart is too weak. Her body is too tormented. You have to understand that she is very, very sick. She will die!" He said.

"If not tomorrow, maybe next week or next month, but she will die."

"I understand," said Elira disappointed. "What option do we have?" she continued.

"You don't have any. Your mother is rotten inside," he tried again to make Elira understand the surgery's gravity. "Look, I'll do my best to keep your mother alive, but the chances are less than 10%."

"I see!" Said Elira. She wasn't upset. How could she be? Somehow, she understood his honesty. She just knew! The medical statistics he provided did not make her give up hope; surprisingly, the ugly truth did not make her cry either.

To Doctor Jack, Liv was already a casualty of life's battles. To Elira, she remained a warrior who always stood up victorious.

"So, tomorrow is the big day. The surgery will last about six hours. I'll call you after." He said, amazed by Elira's optimism.

"Thank you, Doctor Jack. Thank you so much," said Elira sadly.

"Don't thank me yet. Maybe you will have dinner with me sometime," he said, knowing the chances were zero.

When Doctor Jack excused himself and left, Elira called Teo to update her with the latest news.

Teo was very proud of her husband, not only because he admitted that gambling was a problem but also because of his courage to ask for help. Where she thought nothing would save her marriage, destiny proved the contrary.

Cognitive behavioral therapy did not directly help Teo's husband, but it helped him understand that willpower is a significant asset. As he made the first step to recognize his addiction, everything was clear. He engaged in long conversations with Teo and rediscovered the joy of his old hobbies. Recovery from addiction was possible!

When he reached rock bottom, realizing how he had lost a significant amount of money in casinos and almost lost the love of his life, he knew that his addiction was finally over. He was once again enjoying life, and so was Teo.

However, as things were going very well, Teo worried about leaving him alone. She did trust him, but she didn't trust the temptations of gambling, and now, in light of the latest news, she had to decide between her fears and Elira.

Fears scare a lot. Once you are guided by them, you also are lost. Teo knew that, and she had to confront it with intelligence.

To bridge the gap between her apprehensions and her love for her husband, she meticulously organized a romantic dinner. The soft glow of candles illuminated the table, casting a warm ambiance upon the living room.

In the flickering candlelight, she explained her internal struggle. The dinner table became a confessional, where emotions were laid bare in pursuit of understanding.

In Teo's heart, the friendship call sounded louder than her fears. She recognized that Elira needed her support more than her husband required her watchful gaze.

Concluding the conversation, whether or not the issue was entirely settled, Teo and her husband pressed on, determined to save the evening. They continued to relish a delightful dinner, exchanging laughter and playful banter.

As the night progressed, they reached a point where the remnants of their meal stood as a silent witness to the warmth they shared. Leaving the table as it was, they continued the romantic evening in the bedroom.

The following day, Teo packed a few things and left. "Che sera, sera!" she said to herself. Elira was waiting for her.

Elira discovered the hospital building to be a chilling giant, with its nine towering floors resembling a monster in her eyes. Its sheer size and unwelcoming exterior filled anyone who dared to approach with terror. The windows gazed out from the colossal structure, casting a haunting look over the surroundings. Although imposing, the architecture emanated a disconcerting air of desolation, with the pale and lifeless walls conveying institutional coldness accentuated by the harsh lighting. The building, reminiscent of a fortress, projected a shadow of isolation and dread—much more so now that nobody was allowed to enter except medical staff and patients.

In the hushed stillness of her wait, Elira discovered an overwhelming aversion to the incessant wail of ambulances. The shrill sirens clawed at her senses, transporting her back to the haunting image of her mother struggling for breath. It became painfully clear that lingering outside the hospital for hours only intensified her distress.

With little she could do until the surgery concluded, Elira returned home, where Nick, Teo, and her father waited. Doctor Jack had promised her that he would call immediately after the surgery was over.

Hour by hour, Elira found herself treading the delicate path of patience within the confines of the living room. The art of waiting can tip one into madness, especially when a loved one's life hangs in the balance.

The initial six hours stretched into an eternity, each minute burdened with the weight of anticipation. Six hours transformed into eight, then nine, and still, the ominous ring of the phone did not break the oppressive silence.

The house witnessed the collective anxiety and unspoken fright that intensified with each passing moment. The absence of news grew more profound, casting a dark over her once-fleeting optimism that had fueled her endurance.

Elira's father concealed his pain behind the repetitive act of flipping through TV channels as a distraction. Teo, perturbed by the suffocating silence, hesitated to broach any lighthearted conversation. Meanwhile, Nick's worry for his girlfriend etched lines of concern on his face; he believed accepting the facts might ease the burden, yet Elira insisted that Liv embodied a miracle in herself.

Panic took over Elira as she repeatedly dialed Doctor Jack's number, only to be met with an unsettling quiet on the other end. The absence of his response triggered a growth of stress, and for the first time, the haunting possibility crept into her mind—that her mother might not have survived. She was faced with a gloomy possibility, but she couldn't bring herself to fully accept it.

"Darling, think!" Nick said, breaking the silence. "It can't be bad news, can it? You know bad news travels fast. We would have known by now if something went wrong."

"Yes, he's right!" said Teo, happy that someone had broken the silence.

Elira and her father shared a meaningful glance, communicating a mutual understanding. At that precise moment, cutting through the thick tension, a cell phone ringing seized their attention. It was Doctor Jack calling Elira.

Her hands trembled with nervousness as she hastily

answered the call. Every passing second felt like an eternity as the voice on the other end delivered significant news. In the room, an anxious pause hung heavy as the subdued dialogue between the doctor and the patient's daughter played out. Everyone awaited the revelation that would shape their shared destiny.

Can death be a macabre happy ending? Is surviving, without any long future, any kind of life?

It was almost ten hours until the good news. Liv had survived the surgery and was out of danger. However, some important matters needed to be discussed. Doctor Jack preferred to do it in person rather than over the phone, so they arranged to meet at the coffee shop adjacent to the hospital that evening.

Elira chose to take Teo instead of Nick as someone had to stay home with her dad. Fortunately, he was not jealous.

Stepping into the coffee shop, Doctor Jack was taken aback to find not one but two beautiful women awaiting him. The long and demanding yet ultimately successful day had brought him to this moment, where he thought he would combine business with pleasure as a kind of reward.

Elira introduced the doctor to Teo, and despite his attempts to flirt, the conversation quickly shifted to Liv. They had gathered to discuss the post-surgery complications. Now, Doctor Jack had to explain the situation and answer their questions.

"Let me be clear, Elira." He said, "Even if the surgery was a success—I mean a huge success—your mother is not really out of danger."

"What do you mean, Doctor Jack?" Elira asked.

"But you said she's out of danger, didn't you?" added Teo.

"Girls, girls..." he paused. "She was out of complicated post-surgery; she's stable for now. But..."

"I don't get it." Elira interrupted him. "You are telling me she's out of danger, but she's not? How's that possible?"

"Look, as I told you before, your mother is a very, very sick lady. The success of this surgery may give her a few days or months, or maybe years. But she will live in pain. She will not be the same." Doctor Jack tried to convince Elira that, from a medical point of view, Liv didn't have many chances of a normal life.

"Well, doctor, in this day and age, not everyone believes in miracles," said Elira hopefully. "But I do!" She continued, "You don't know my mother; she's a fighter and under God's protection. Otherwise, according to medical statistics, she would have been in Heaven by now."

Amazed, again, by her optimism and more by how her best friend thought exactly like Elira on the matter, Doctor Jack felt obliged to insist on preparing her for the worst. He also brought into the discussion, as an excuse, the money he took for the surgery. He was likely ensuring he could not be involved in a corruption scandal.

He couldn't manipulate Elira, so he came up with the idea of allowing her to visit Liv in the hospital. And how could she refuse the opportunity to see her mom? She had to commit a crime and be punished with three months in jail if caught. Doctor Jack had her! In this way, as an illegality, Elira couldn't sue him.

Everything was planned in detail, and Elira was very happy. The next day, she had to go to the hospital's back entrance and wait for a male nurse to bring her a stethoscope and a doctor's white coat.

To enter the hospital, she had to disguise herself as a doctor. She knew it was wrong, but she wanted to see her mother so much. She also knew Doctor Jack was exposing her to blackmail if necessary, but she didn't care!

With maximum fear, she joined this illegal game, and now she was a delinquent, too!

It was a cold winter day, and the crisp air brought back memories of Elira's childhood Christmases spent in the mountains with her parents.

Those memories were good for her. She no longer thought about the ugly image of the hospital's backyard that could be seen from behind the barrier at the entrance, nor about the medical staff walking the alleys with coffees and cigarettes in hand, a smug satisfaction on their faces. The epidemic had been a boon to them—a break from the prying eyes of patients' families, a rare freedom they relished.

An uncategorized species of homo sapiens worked there, people with no soul, without any mercy, without any respect. How some people undergo a drastic change while at work is a mystery. They were like monsters, treating people with hatred. But, as soon as their shift ends, they become loving mothers, sisters, wives, friends, and so on. It's perplexing how a profession that requires kindness and compassion can bring out such evil in some individuals.

Despite being instructed by Doctor Jack to arrive at noon, she found herself waiting alone at the gate. A delay like this can cause unnecessary frustration for anyone. After an hour, the security lady became suspicious, or was it just Elira's imagination?

Ten minutes later, she noticed a thin man with a large bag approaching in the distance. He first went to the security lady, chatting and laughing with her for a while, and then he walked over to Elira.

He introduced himself as Gabriel. He seemed very young for this job, almost a boy. He was friendly, which was a relief to Elira. He calmly told her to not be afraid because nobody would ask her anything. The hospital was too big, and nobody cared about other people's business.

Elira had to pay the security lady, the elevator operator, and Gabriel. And that was just the beginning!

Once they reached the seventh floor, Elira's heart accelerated. She had to think of something beautiful, like her childhood vacations, to not show her mother any negative emotions.

As she strolled down the corridor, she was pleasantly surprised by its pristine cleanliness. The linoleum floors gleamed, and the walls radiated a freshly whitewashed brilliance. The nurses' station was positioned in the middle of the corridor while the doctors' offices lined the far end. Room 2020, her mother's, awaited as the sixth door on the right, directly opposite the nurses' station.

Elira couldn't help but catch the subdued whispers among the nurses as she approached the door of 2020. It now dawned on her why Doctor Jack had advised against conversing with them. The tension left no doubt about the shared unease that gripped the place.

Emotionally unbalanced, Elira had experienced a blend of happiness and sadness. She found herself once again struck by the immaculate cleanliness of the room. It was a solitary space with a generous window providing ample light. A small TV, likely broken, sat quietly in the upper-right corner. A lone bedside cabinet stood on the right side of Liv's bed. Liv lay there, looking pale, with an IV that seemed to disturb her, lost in a deep slumber. She couldn't fathom the presence of her daughter.

Gabriel softly tried to wake Liv, informing her that her

daughter had arrived. Due to the anesthesia, Liv felt a sense of confusion that was particularly difficult to deal with. Maintaining mental clarity was crucial for her recovery. Still, the medication seemed to take it away.

"Hi, Mom. How do you feel?" Elira said with love and mercy. "Why are you wearing the mask here, Mom?" she continued.

"They told me to," answered Liv sadly.

"Why did she have to wear the mask? She can't breathe, for God's sake!". Elira addressed to Gabriel. "Where is Doctor Jack?"

"I don't know. I'm going to call the nurse in charge." He said, leaving the room.

"Elira, please don't make a scene," said Liv. "Why don't you help me to turn on the other side, could you?"

In these circumstances, at her mother's request, Elira had to be polite and not argue with any nurse or Doctor Jack. After all, for better or for worse, he was the one who gave her access to the hospital. Otherwise, who knew if she could see her mother again.

The evident agony Liv experienced turned it into a genuine struggle, with each movement causing discomfort throughout her body. Elira, hesitant and fearful of causing her mother more pain, had to find a solution. How? She was too afraid to touch Liv. How could she help her mother without hurting her?

"Honey, use the sheet. Pull it towards you a bit, then roll me over," Liv said, relieving her daughter.

Liv's idea was surprisingly effective. Elira struggled to lift the weight, straining her arms and back. But, as they say, a supernatural force gives you strength in these cases.

Before falling asleep again, Liv told her daughter to be careful around there, and she advised her not to come to visit anymore. The law was the law! Besides, rumors had said that many medical staff members were already infected.

Elira fixed her eyes at the woman who had cheated death once again, her hero. Her miracle! In silent gratitude, she repeatedly thanked God for each time He saved her mother.

Liv, opting for assistance from strangers, jeopardized her own well-being to ensure Elira's safety. Yet, a question persisted—was the flu epidemic truly the root of the problem, or was something far more sinister at play, hidden beneath the surface? The profound truth of Liv's care and her quiet efforts for Elira stirred a deep, emotional response. Elira would find out the real reason later.

While Liv was sleeping, a nurse came by to check her vitals and explain to Elira why her mother was required to wear a mask. The nurse, who was less friendly than Gabriel, conveyed the information straightforward yet politely. Elira was skeptical and didn't fully accept the explanation, as she recognized the mask as an internal hospital protocol rather than a necessary measure.

Elira decided not to cause trouble for her mom's sake and tried to ignore the nurse. However, she had a feeling that something was off. Checking Liv's vital signs took longer than expected, even though everything seemed under control. Soon enough, Elira realized what the nurse was actually doing.

As Elira approached the nurse to put some money in her pocket, she noticed the technique of attracting the attention of those in question by placing the pen vertically and keeping the pocket open.

Otherwise, what else could a nurse with no desire to

work do next to a sleeping patient who did not require her services?

Four other nurses on duty came to check Liv's vital signs that day. It was the same ritual, the same thing, and the same money.

With her generosity, Elira innocently thought that the nurses would pay special attention to her mother through this gesture. *Innocently!*

XIV

A week after the surgery, Liv started to act weird. In her moments of lucidity, after each visit of Elira, she heard the gossip of the nurses, speculating about a love affair between her daughter and Doctor Jack. If they weren't gossiping about a so-called adventure, they were commenting that Elira wore jeans or sneakers, and despite this style of clothing, no one had noticed that she was an intruder. All this affected Liv, especially since she was not recovering after the surgery.

With no other option, Elira reluctantly accepted her mother's decision. She could no longer visit the hospital or speak with Doctor Jack. From that point on, any news would come through Liv. But Elira wasn't satisfied. Despite his repeated requests to meet, she continued to stay in touch with Doctor Jack, though only by phone. She never saw him again.

Confused by last week's routine, she felt useless. She thought of her mother alone in that hospital room, surrounded by those creatures called nurses. And yet, she felt she had a trustworthy man on the inside, giving her hope.

Gabriel turned out to be a good person. Even though he had to be paid, at least he was helpful. Whatever Elira asked him to do, he did. Liv, too, was comfortable with him.

Time passed, and there were no signs of improvement. Liv wanted to go home. She didn't want to stay in the hospital anymore. She now often got angry with Elira for leaving her there. Although she didn't feel well, sometimes she didn't even have the strength to speak. She just wanted to go home with all her might. Elira started to carefully investigate what it would take to bring her mother home, weighing the risks and implications of such a decision.

Fear! She was more afraid than ever of losing her mother. Of course, Liv was not well in the hospital, but at home? Who would take care of her? Neither she nor her father had the necessary medical training to take this huge risk. And yet, could you ignore a mother's wish?

When all efforts seemed meaningless, the only option was to weigh the pros and cons of the situation. So, after the usual dinner, Elira invited her father, Teo, and Nick to the living room for a glass of wine.

"I think we should bring mom home." Elira started.

"Why?" Teo said. "She's too sick, Elira," she continued.

"I don't know. Maybe I will find a private nurse." Elira said.

"Bring her home, sweetie." Elira's father said sadly, leaving the room.

"Okay, darling, call Doctor Jack," Nick said.

Teo disagreed, but only Liv knew precisely what she was going through and what was best for her. Who were they to oppose this requirement? And if she was to die, she had to die in her own home. Maybe she was too tired to fight anymore. Elira refused to accept that her mother's death was merely a release from pain.

She needed the doctor's approval, which was easy to obtain. Doctor Jack could only grant the request if Liv signed the hospital discharge papers. He made it clear he had no intention of prolonging her mother's stay. It wasn't favorable for his career to keep a patient post-surgery for an extended period.

The flu epidemic had gotten worse, and the only safe place for Liv was where she was; even if she had to die, it was better to die in the hospital. According to the latest directives from the Ministry of Health, anyone who died at home, in an ambulance, or in the emergency room, regardless of the actual cause, had to have the flu listed as the cause of death on the death certificate.

Discussing certain matters over the phone was dangerous, and sharing information could have resulted in Doctor Jack losing his license or even going to prison. Despite this, he felt compelled to tell Elira the truth, even though he did not fully understand why. He was surprised by his own reaction and did not recognize himself anymore.

Among his words were profound messages that Elira refused to listen to. She knew that the epidemic had gotten more and more complicated. She knew that the restrictions had worsened. It was a massive media scandal because those who died of the flu no longer had the right to a decent burial.

The hospital authorities buried the flu victims in black plastic bags without clothes and directly transported them to the cemetery. They prohibited the ceremony in the church, which caused immense pain to the bereaved.

Liv cared about traditions; she believed in God, Christian rituals, superstitions, and things from Orthodox culture, such as if dying without a lighted candle condemned one to darkness in the afterlife, symbolizing the eternal interplay between light and shadow. Worse, she couldn't imagine a funeral without the church funeral ceremony; only the suicides, considered sinners, did not have this right.

Since she was a little girl, Elira often heard this story about those who took their own lives. Her mother had this combination of pity and fear at the same time as she told what a terrible sin suicide was. At that time, Elira could not understand why these people, pushed by who knew what force, thought, or pain, did not have the right to a funeral like everyone else had.

Certain priests said that no cross should have been placed at their graves either because they did not carry the hardships of their lives to the end. They did not accept their cross as our Lord Jesus Christ.

Sin! A big sin, but wasn't it God who forgave all our sins?! Didn't suicidal people, through their cruel acts, need God's love more than anyone else?

Liv didn't want that; she was not a suicide! She fought too hard to stay alive, and she suffered unimaginable pain. There were days when maybe death would have been a better solution, yet she refused to accept it.

Without going into too many details, Elira explained to her mother why coming home was dangerous. She needed to be careful and avoid misunderstanding, as Liv became extremely sensitive.

The following day, a cold Thursday, Elira had a long conversation with her mother via video call. Liv seemed to be better; the news didn't bother her so much, and she accepted that staying in the hospital was a good decision until things calmed down.

Was she healing? Liv hadn't been in such a good mood for a long time. Or was she pretending so as not to upset her daughter?

Although happy to see her mother in a positive state, Elira's intuition said otherwise, and after finishing the conversation, she immediately called Gabriel to ask what was happening with her mother. Gabriel kept her up to date with absolutely every movement and every change regarding Liv.

Liv's attitude looked strange to him, too, because overnight, she had a seizure, and they had to keep her on oxygen for a few hours, then they gave her sedatives. But not knowing Liv well, he thought the sedatives made her feel better.

Gabriel told Elira that he would work twelve hours that day and make sure Liv hadn't missed anything, advising Elira to rest, relax, and do something for herself.

She thanked Gabriel for being so kind and thought hanging out with Teo, and Nick would be nice. Poor them; they left their needs aside to support Elira. For Nick, it was alright; he was busy with work all the time, but Teo had nothing else to do.

She was far from her husband and often wondered if he would be strong enough without her if he had to be. She also missed him a lot, but her best friend was going through tough times. So, Elira's invitation came as a blessing.

The three of them had lunch together. They joked and laughed. It was pleasant. Nick was happy to see his girlfriend smiling again. He adored her. He wanted the moment to last forever but had to excuse himself to finish a work project, leaving the two friends to enjoy their time at the shops.

"Have you had nightmares lately?" Teo asked as soon as

Nick left.

"Yes, but I didn't want to upset you anymore," answered Elira.

"Come on, you know I'm crazy about your dreams," said Teo, disappointed that her best friend did not share her dreams.

"Yes, yes, I know! There's nothing new to reveal. Actually, I have the same nightmare, but it's a little different. Anyway, you are always present in my dreams and always wear the same pink socks," said Elira, smiling.

In fact, Elira had the same nightmare very often, with small, unimportant details changed. But not the socks!

Going from one store to another, buying things they didn't need for fun, they decided to decipher the meaning of the socks from the big nightmare—or instead, Teo would decode it while Elira listened and nodded in agreement.

After analyzing the color pink and the fact that only Teo wore socks, they finally concluded that it represented the connection between reality and fantasy. During the chaos of Elira's dream, where she was unsure of her world, the pink socks were a clear indication of fantasy. The answer! Teo tried to open Elira's eyes to the truth in that nightmare. By wearing them, she was the key!

It was a lovely day, and after finishing their shopping, they went back home to play backgammon while enjoying a cup of coffee. They played until just before dinner. However, something suddenly changed when Elira listened to her mother's latest voicemail. She began to feel sick.

"That's it! Oh God!" said Elira, crying.

"Elira, calm down. What's happened?" said Teo, worried about Elira. A few minutes ago, her best friend laughed and joked, and now she couldn't pull herself together.

Something terrible must have happened.

"Teo, you must leave," said Elira, trying to stop crying.

"Why? What's wrong?" asked Teo surprisingly.

"Okay, Okay, I have to calm down. You call Nick, I'm going to find my dad," said Elira.

When they all gathered, Elira told them she would bring Liv home the following day, against the doctor's advice. Without much explanation, she made them listen to her mother's voicemail.

Liv could barely speak, and the desperation could be heard in her weak voice. It was unclear if she was crying; probably yes, but what she asked in the message was like a last wish—the only wish, a beg!

Drama, tragedy, sadness, end! The most painful voice message ever lasted for precisely one minute, one minute to break a heart. Liv said, pausing often to breathe: "I want to go home... It's this stupid shift...that makes me want to go home...Our Father...which... art in ...Heaven... Hallowed by thy name..." Then, after finishing all the prayer, she concluded: "It's an ordeal! It's an ordeal!"

Everyone was astonished. It was evident that Liv's request arose due to a lack of care, even if Elira kept offering money without hesitation. She was so generous that, in her imagination, it seemed like she had to give money to every person she met on the street. Even when she stopped visiting her mother, she sent money through Gabriel to pay for Liv's "expenses." The financial aspect was well handled, as the bribe had to be paid. Yet, something was wrong! The level of corruption was extraordinarily high and unacceptable.

XV

Bidding farewell to everyone, Teo departed that evening as Elira had requested. At first, she was puzzled about why she had to leave, especially since they were bringing Liv home. Soon, she realized that the main reason was to reduce the risk of Liv catching for the second time the flu. With fewer people around, there would be less chance of infection.

Teo was returning home, Nick would stay in the new apartment, and Liv would only be cared for by Elira and her father.

At half past seven on Friday morning, Elira called the hospital to arrange an ambulance. She avoided calling Doctor Jack; she was too upset with his team, the nurses, and even Gabriel. Liv's voice message wasn't a lie or an illusion. Liv suffered not only from her illness but also from disrespect and insensitivity on the part of human beings whose job it is to take care of the sick to relieve their pain, both physical and mental. Things would have been different if the medical system had been clean. Maybe Liv would have been cured if the nurses had helped her recover. But it's just a maybe! Unfortunately, the reality was different. Liv, very sick, was going to continue her suffering at home. Perhaps her way back to life!

The paperwork and ambulance transport arrangements were made before lunchtime. During this time, Liv had called Elira a few times, asking when she would be home. Her voice was weak; she stammered, and she was not coherent. However, Elira maintained her optimism that her mother would be much better at home no matter what happened. The bond between a mother and a child is a miracle worker, and Elira relied on this to help her mother heal.

Liv arrived home in the afternoon, and what was supposed to bring hope turned into torment. She looked terrible; her appearance was nothing short of alarming. Her face bore the telltale signs of excessive swelling, her body marred by bruises and punctures, and her skin was extremely dry. In moments, it became clear that Liv's poor condition was due to medical negligence.

Reading the discharge letter signed by Doctor Jack, Elira discovered that her mom had nine diseases at that point. She knew about three; how could a person live with nine diseases?

Elira was just seven years old when her mom was diagnosed with SLE (Systemic lupus erythematosus), an autoimmune disease in which the immune system attacks its tissues, causing widespread inflammation and tissue damage in the affected organs. But all she could remember was the haunting, agonizing scream of her mother, a sound that scratched her mind like a curse.

Liv discovered that she suffered from this incurable disease when she went to the doctor with pain at the tips of her fingers caused by coin-shaped tissue growing under the nails. Everyone thought it was a nasty infection, but then the results came, and for Liv, a terror!

Growing up, Elira started to ask questions about her mother's disease. She read that lupus has no known cure and only an appropriate treatment can keep the disease under control.

Liv already knew that! She began gathering information about the potential risks she might face, and her daughter did, too. Despite feeling anxious, she knew she needed to create a solid plan for her family's well-being and happiness.

After a few years of being diagnosed, Liv began experiencing more severe symptoms, and her health condition was getting worse day by day. Everybody was in shock after the test results! Primary diagnosis: Systemic lupus erythematosus involving organs or systems with articular, skin, and hematological immunological manifestations. Secondary diagnoses: Idiopathic thrombocytopenic purpura, a rare autoimmune disorder; the blood doesn't clot properly because the immune system destroys the blood-clotting platelets.

There was too much medical information for a child, and it terrified Elira. It marked the beginning of her nightmares as she poured over medical articles she barely understood. Liv had no idea about Elira's research. If only she had known!

The doctors explained to Liv that having two diseases active simultaneously can be fatal. They reassured her that a new treatment could put one disease to sleep when the other was active and vice versa. They advised her to follow the treatment properly to avoid complications, so she did. Then heart problems appeared, followed by a double bypass, and so on, until the day when Liv could no longer get out of bed.

Elira reread the discharge letter; she was now angry. The ninth disease was E. coli post-surgery, once again suggesting medical negligence. She decided not to share her disappointment with her father; instead, she planned to not let Liv alone for even a second. They were going to take care of her in shifts.

Elira's optimism and pessimism juggled like tennis balls. When hope was at its peak, everything seemed solvable; when hope disappeared, everything was dark—just dark!

Tired and seriously ill, Liv was finally sleeping peacefully in her bed at home. Elira had tried to find a private nurse, but no one wanted to take responsibility. It was too complicated, a very difficult job—nobody wanted to dare the scythe's servant.

"Dad, it's just you and me!" said Elira.

"Not surprised," he said. "You stay with your mother, and I'm going to cook something for all of us," he continued.

"I wa... I wan... want sausage," said Liv from the bed.

"Mom, you are awake!"

"I'm going to make sausage," said Elira's father.

"Dad..." Elira was concerned about her mother's food request.

"No, Elira, not now! We are going to give her whatever she wants."

He went to cook sausage as Liv asked while Elira cleaned her mother with a soft, wet towel. Liv was in pain, although Elira barely touched her.

Elira's plan to care for her mother failed! Liv started to be agitated; she couldn't sleep well, and every five to ten minutes, she wanted to be turned over to the other side as she couldn't find a comfortable position.

Helping her change position was a challenge; the only

way to do that was to use the sheet and roll her on the side she wanted. It worked until Elira's father fell asleep.

Around four o'clock on Saturday morning, as the eerie stillness enveloped the house, Elira grappled with the daunting task of changing her mother's position. Exhaustion gnawed at her with every effort, threatening to engulf her. In a sudden, overwhelming wave, Elira crashed. She knew they were untenable to continue that way; they needed more medical expertise for Liv.

Liv had brief moments of clarity during the night, which gave her daughter the courage to continue. Elira didn't even know how to administer the medicine. Liv was the only one who knew. But the other moments were macabre, such as when Liv repeatedly called out "Father."

Was she calling her daughter's father? Perhaps it was a cry for help, a plea for him to assume the role of a parent rather than a husband. Nonetheless, there was an unmistakable sense of peculiarity surrounding them.

Somehow, Elira found a sense of relief in uncertainty. Memories of her grandmother's final days flooded her mind, mainly when she repeatedly uttered "Mama." It was an experience that profoundly impacted Elira, one that she later came to understand. In the throes of death's agony, when the end draws near, it's often the mother's name that escapes the lips of many. It's as if, in the circle of life, we return to the source from which we began. For Elira's grandmother, the yearning for a mother figure in her last moments was all too understandable since she was an orphan.

Unexpectedly, Elira's mind was disturbed by thoughts overshadowed by sadness. Could her mother be dying? Is Liv calling her dead father? Or is she calling out to God?

She didn't know what to believe anymore; she was tired, and she had pain in her arms and back caused by the action of turning her mother from side to side. Once again, with great effort, she banished her negative thoughts. She made coffee and started cleaning around when her father started to talk.

"She's dying," he said.

"Don't say that."

"Oh, Elira, you are not a child anymore! I know it is hard but look at her. Look at her!" he paused for a second, "Do you think she wants to live like this?"

"You're right, Dad; I will call Dr. Paula in the morning," Elira answered her father.

The unimaginable happened around lunchtime, as Liv's body betrayed her all at once, spiraling into a rapid, terrifying decline. She turned blue, and every breath became a desperate struggle. Unable to ask for help, she suffocated in silence, her eyes pleading for salvation.

In a panic, Elira dashed outside to find an ambulance, Liv's life dangling in the balance, slipping away with each passing moment. Fortunately, the siren's wail broke the agony within five minutes—a miraculous stroke of luck. As the paramedics raced against time, Elira, with trembling hands, implored them to save her mother.

The doctor urgently demanded immediate transportation to the hospital. Liv, wrapped in a simple purple blanket, was swiftly taken away without her belongings—no phone, no purse, no medications. Tears streamed down Elira's face as her mother's desperate plea, "Don't leave me alone," reverberated in her mind with a haunting dread. She could hardly bear to watch as they placed Liv into the ambulance, her heart wrenching with each passing second.

The first and last time, Elira couldn't catch her instinct; it was as if she had none. A deep, soul-crushing hurt tore through her beyond anything imaginable—a pain she knew no one else had ever felt. And she was right. Yet, through the veil of tears, she strained to hear a premonition that didn't exist. Desperately, she clung to the flicker of hope that had always guided her. But this time, it felt hollow. After all, if her mother was truly meant to die, didn't the bloodline demand she feel it first?

Overcome with anguish, Elira's father remained by Liv's side until the ambulance's back doors closed. He was a silent watcher in the wake of uncertainty, his heart weighed down by fear and a sense of powerlessness. Crying, he said, "She died."

XVI

Wet to the skin and cold, Elira made her way through towering buildings in an unfamiliar neighborhood within the bustling metropolis. She had no idea where she was, simply allowing her instincts to guide her. Liv had been confined to the hospital for nearly two months, and amidst the ongoing epidemic, their only means of communication had been through cell phones and messengers. Now, she vanished like she never existed.

She called her mom several times and left messages without an answer. She also called the hospital and Dr. Paula, but it was like they never existed.

Nothing could halt Elira's determination; she continued calling her mother and sending messages. Nick tried to convince her to return home and rest, assuring her they would visit all the hospitals in town the following day. Elira couldn't understand how Nick had found her, but she felt relieved that she wasn't alone despite her anger.

"She'd never have vanished on me. Something horrible happened," Elira said to Nick.

She felt inclined to heed Nick's advice significantly as the rain intensified, drenching her further and sending chills down her spine. At that precise moment, the familiar video chat ringtone of the messenger application echoed through Elira's phone. The image of her mother appeared in a small circle on the screen, filling Elira's heart with indescribable joy.

"Oh, Elira, how many times have I told you not to disturb me? I am okay," Liv said.

She appeared surprisingly well, almost as if she had never been ill. Elira's heart raced with fear at this unexpected sight, and she urgently questioned Liv about her whereabouts. However, all Liv could offer was vague information about being transferred to another hospital, unable to identify the location. Despite Elira's concern, Liv reassured her daughter not to worry, insisting she felt perfectly fine.

Understanding that her daughter continued not to believe her, as proof, she showed her hand with infusion, bringing it closer to the camera in such a way as to indicate the points marked with colored dots on the extensor tendons, explaining that with trivial vitamins injected into the respective points they healed her.

Was it a miracle? Elira couldn't help but entertain the thought. A strange feeling gnawed at her insides. Despite her desire to believe in the phenomenal transformation before her, doubts remained at the edges of her mind. Yet, she pushed those doubts aside and longed to embrace the sight before her: her mother, restored to perfect health, exuding beauty and radiance. What more could she possibly wish for?

Still, Elira, as a final confirmation, driven by a shadow of mental restlessness, begged Liv to at least tell her the doctor's name.

"Give it up, Elira," said Liv. "Don't bother Ms. Doctor. She's taking good care of me. Stop looking for answers," she continued.

"Mom, please! You have to give me something!" said Elira. "Ask a nurse at what hospital you are. Ask the doctor's name," she insisted.

Then, with an indescribable calm emanating from a divine peace of mind devoid of pain, Liv says: "Ms. Doctor Death has healed me!"

Elira knew the precise time the ambulance departed with her mother: 4:47 PM. She couldn't have been mistaken. As the ambulance doors slammed shut, fragments of her last nightmare flashed through her mind. Perhaps the answer she was looking for, the lost instinct, the premonition, was hidden within the dream, but her sadness kept her from grasping it. A fragile hope was left, and she dialed Nick's number as she needed him more than ever.

The doctor instructed her to await the hospital's call while the nurse assured them that her mother would not perish. Yet, the prolonged wait lasted until midnight when Elira's cell phone finally rang. It was the hospital. A young woman's voice conveyed to Elira that her mother was very ill, intubated in the CCU, and for the time being, they could only wait helplessly. Elira's breath caught in her throat. "It's happening again," she whispered to herself.

Crushed by the last news, Elira, drained by the constant agony gnawing at her mind and heart, finally surrendered to a fitful sleep, where even her dreams brought no relief from the suffocating misery.

The next morning, Elira's cell phone cracked the silence and woke her up. On the other end, a chillingly indifferent woman's voice delivered the devastating news—Liv had departed this world at six o'clock that morning. Cause of death: flu.

What followed was beyond words. Elira's father, having lit a candle, retreated to the garden to mourn silently. Nick was consoling Elira while Teo was on her way back. Elira grappled with disbelief—how had she not foreseen this? Guilt consumed her, a relentless burden on her soul. She seethed with anger at herself for failing; she should have taken better care of her mom. And then, the impending funeral struck her like a blow to the chest.

What had she feared her entire life had now come to pass. Liv departed this world alone, devoid of the comfort of a lighted candle as per Orthodox tradition. And now, she was destined to be laid to rest in a black trash bag, denied the honor of a proper funeral service, not in the church! She was relegated to the fate of those who committed suicide. It was a cruel injustice. Liv, who had fought tirelessly for life, enduring unimaginable physical agony and carrying her cross until the very end, was denied the dignity and respect owed to her in death.

The first step Elira took was to contact Gabriel, offering a significant sum of money to secure a connection at the morgue. Yet, no one dared take the risk for what Elira requested.

All she looked for was a shred of humanity, someone within who could at least clothe Liv's body. They didn't care about Elira's mom when she was alive, so why should they care for her now that she's dead? Ultimately, it seemed money couldn't buy everything, even if Gabriel did his best.

Elira didn't give up; she contacted a lawyer, yet again, with no results. Then she turned to the funeral director for help, only to face severe restrictions that left Liv destined to be buried naked.

Finally, with no other options left, Elira, through tears, had to take charge of the funeral arrangements. All she had to do was obtain the authorization to bury her mother.

Until then, Liv's body had been trapped in a container outside the morgue.

There were six large containers, each with shelves on the right and left, holding bodies in black plastic bags. It was a horrifying sight, and yet, what harm could a dead body do? Doesn't infection die with the person? Why keep them there?

Even if there was nothing after death, even if, once someone died, the pain died too. Even if a dead body was just a dead body, the suffering of those left behind was always terrible.

Perhaps all this had nothing to do with the epidemic; maybe it was a dirty political game to control the population.

Teo arrived on Monday morning, ready to support Elira. Nick was also there, offering his presence and comfort. Teo accompanied Elira everywhere: the hospital, the police station, the mayor's office, and the church. Both of them were constantly in tears. The concern of not being able to arrange a funeral for their loss created a dangerous mix of emotions that they struggled to control.

The funeral was scheduled for Wednesday at 1:00 p.m. With no chance of a regular ceremony, Elira felt a mounting fear as she rushed from one office to another in hopes of obtaining the burial authorization in time. Liv was already gone, so why was there such a delay in signing the death certificate? Desperate, Elira resorted to calling the police to intervene and resolve the bureaucratic hurdles.

On the morning of the funeral, she met with an inspector who could assist her. It was a race against time; they had to be at the cemetery by one o'clock. The inspector managed to negotiate with the morgue officials, finally securing Liv's death certificate. With a sense of relief, albeit fleeting, Elira hailed a taxi. Now, they could proceed with the funeral arrangements. She had permission!

Sitting on the back seat of the taxi, trying to hold back her tears, Elira glanced at the piece of paper in her hand. Reading it, she cried hysterically, startling the taxi driver. She couldn't believe what she was reading; Elira was in shock. Her mother had passed away on Sunday morning at six o'clock, so why did the death certificate state a time of death at 4:47 PM on Friday? Was her mother already dead when the hospital claimed she was intubated? Could it have been a mistake? But the timing was too precise, exactly like when the ambulance had taken Liv away forever.

Her father's account echoed in her mind; he had witnessed her passing, yet they were made to believe she was alive for several long hours afterward.

She was consumed by anger, consumed by the desire to bury her mother and then take legal action against the entire hospital—doctors, nurses, the entire system. It was a stark contrast to her usual manner. But she soon realized that such a battle would be lengthy and costly, offering no good to her mother's departed soul. Nick later guided her to understand better, as he often did, with calmness and love, helping Elira work through the challenges and choose the best path forward.

The first months following the funeral were devastating for Elira; her world had undergone a dramatic change. Lost in remorse, she retreated within her home, distancing herself from Nick and Teo. Fortunately, her father found comfort in tending to the garden daily, becoming the first to return to his routine. He understood that his beloved wife, though departed, had found peace.

Elira needed more time; in the other world, Liv was happy, transformed into an angel, a saint.

XVII

"Ms. Doctor Death has healed me," and Elira woke up. She had the same nightmare before Liv died. A year after her mom passed away, why the same dream? What does it mean? Yet now she wished to keep dreaming, be it a nightmare or anything that could make her see her mother. Elira was already forgetting everything that had happened in her dreams; it was fading away as a breath in a mirror. She hated that; she always wanted to remember! Even if hers were often nightmares. She tried to hold on to dreams, but they always slipped through her fingers. The only place to meet her mother again was the world of fantasy, the dream world, a liminal space, the great beyond, but not the afterlife.

It was a challenging year. Elira was immersed in remorse, and she often felt guilty. Although she used to dream about her mother every night, dreams with specific meaning, answers to the pain, and answers on how to move on, she still couldn't let go of Liv. Elira needed more time!

Teo felt blessed, almost astonished at how much difference one year could make in life. From pain, bitterness, tragedy, and unrelenting heartbreak, she had turned around to face a new beginning, a new life!

Happy and pregnant now, Teo left her best friend to grieve on her own terms. Nick too! Poor him; as much as

Elira tried not to show him the painful chaos she lived in, he just knew!

Lucky was Elira's father when, two months after his wife passed away, he found an abandoned little puppy. Gardening with his new buddy made his days easier to live. That dog changed how he grieved so positively that he also considered finding one for his daughter. He left the idea to be discussed at Liv's first death anniversary. But Teo had a better plan—a surprise!

Teo miraculously kept the key that could open Elira's door to leave the world of grief. Everyone already knew about Teo's pregnancy, but no one knew if it was a boy or a girl.

After Liv's departure, Elira made sure that the third, sixth, and ninth memorial services were performed in the church, and the Trisagion at the cemetery. For one year, the same things happened: the same Orthodox rituals, the same church, the same priest, and the same cemetery for the same beloved person. It was a must for her, whether she believed it or not. Everything had to be done according to Liv's wishes.

The memorial was quite ordinary. Elira, in tears, asked the priest once again if they had done everything correctly. She was terrified of forgetting some important tradition. The reproaches weighed heavily on her. As she looked around, she saw Nick; he appeared sad, probably at his limits. How could she have ignored him all this time? How had she let grief take over her life in such a way? Then she realized how fortunate she was. No one else would ever stand by her as Nick had. "Oh God, what have I done to him?" murmured Elira to herself.

It had been a hard day for everyone, but fortunately, it ended on a positive note at Elira's father's house, where they gathered for dinner.

"How are you doing, my dear child?" Elira's father asked while petting his dog.

"I will not lie, Dad," Elira answered, thinking how lucky she was to have such a beautiful family, including Teo and her husband. I have my dark days. I suppose everybody does. I miss her..." and she was interrupted by Teo.

"I have something very important to tell you, so please, may I have your attention?" Teo looked much more beautiful than she was; her happiness shone brightly.

As all waited to hear what was so important, Elira experienced a déjà vu, something even more intense. She felt and saw, in precise detail, exactly what was about to happen. She knew every word, pause, breath, and action Teo would make. Her mood shifted from sadness to joy, and with a smile, she urged Teo not to keep them waiting and to share the good news.

"You know, don't you?" asked Teo.

"Go ahead, I know nothing!" Elira said, amused.

"Oh, come on! It's not fair!" Teo said, now almost disappointed.

"Girls, girls..." Nick stopped them.

"Alright, I am pregnant, of course," Teo said, pointing to the big belly, enjoying the amusement in the room, "And as you already know, Elira will baptize my child," emotions overwhelmed her, "And it's a girl!" she concluded fast as she couldn't keep up the suspense anymore.

It was as if the day's pain had magically turned into joy —death into life! Yet, according to Elira's déjà vu, there was more of a surprise to come. After the commotion caused by the wonderful news, Teo turned to her soul sister, took Elira's hands, and continued softly, "I will name my baby Liv."

Silence, tears, happiness, and a future! This was the point at which Elira ended her mourning and returned to reality. The baby girl needed her.

When it was just the two of them, Teo asked Elira if she had any interesting dreams. "I need something to think about and do," she said.

"Okay. I've been having weird dreams. They're more like memories, although they are not."

"Love it! Love it! Say more!" said Teo exited.

"Honey, I don't think it's a good idea. I mean, look at you! You're pregnant!" Elira said, worried about not harming her friend. "You should think about little Liv now, not my dreams." But at Teo's insistence, she relented.

A pregnant woman and her best friend couldn't sleep that night. They discussed the meanings and confusions of dreams, visions, and feelings.

An unforgettable evening, maybe even a bridge to what is a life. At least for Elira, one way or another, she had to get her feet back on the ground. Otherwise, what good is all the pain collected, all the tears shed? Was Liv coming back? Could this intense mourning make Liv's transition to the light easier? Or worse? All these questions no longer made sense. Elira had to focus on her life and that of her family. Her mother would continue to live on in memories or even in imagination, as she had over the past year.

When Elira couldn't see her mother in her dreams, she sensed her presence everywhere. She was sure of what she felt, even if it was invisible. *A sign!*

At dawn, they went to bed, but Elira could not sleep. Thoughts, plans, a mixture of bitter and sweet, or perhaps the fear of leaving the past in the past and focusing on the future. After all, she had no reason to be so miserable; she lacked absolutely nothing. Moreover, she had unconditional love from everyone around her. What else is more powerful? What else could be more important? Isn't love the ultimate weapon against the evil that surrounds us? She often looked for the answers to these questions, even though she already knew them. Somehow, if she didn't stop now, she would become selfish, ultimately hurting those who loved her.

A long time ago, Elira created her forever little corner of Heaven, a peaceful place like something from a fairy tale. It was a way of disconnecting, transitioning from awake to falling asleep. She felt peace of mind, total relief, and an ultimate refuge in that place. From there to dreams, she couldn't explain the way.

It was the most beautiful, picturesque landscape. Away from reality, Elira felt herself with spirit lying on a checkered blanket on flawless green grass, facing a clean, crystal-clear river flowing calmly at the feet of tall mountains, which were also wrapped in green.

There, in that magical place, she was surrounded by many lovely rabbits. From way above, she heard the birds chirping. Looking up, she could admire the majestic peaks of the mountains touching the perfect blue sky, covered with white clouds resembling angels. It was her place, a kind of Paradise with many flowers of all colors scattered here and there. Elira never came back directly from that place to reality. She had to cross the world of sleep first.

Something changed once with Liv's death!

Elira could no longer stay in her imaginary place during

the mourning period. At first, she felt a presence. How was it possible? It was a place she created; someone else was not allowed there. It was her mind!

Along the way, that presence shaped like a silhouette at the river's edge. With her back to Elira, dressed in black, Liv stared blankly at the river or the mountains— Elira couldn't tell. Her mother was there, in her corner of Paradise. Nothing else mattered. Elira remained on the blanket, simply watching and waiting, overjoyed to see her mother, even if she couldn't see her face. After a while, Liv began to turn her head towards Elira. The pain was evident, like a draw on her face. Pain after death? Could that even have been possible? Or perhaps it wasn't pain at all, but something more sinister—worry, cloaked in the guise of pain. Maybe anguish pressed on her because Elira hadn't allowed her the peace of an eternal rest. After death, there was another life where the living had no place. Yet the bond between the dead and the living could be perilously powerful, holding consequences for both. The grief tethered to this world would have had to cease to let Liv's soul finally rest.

The last time Elira went to the magic place, after a slow goodbye, Liv turned her head towards Elira and smiled — a smile that spoke of happiness, and Elira knew! Liv had found her eternal resting place.

Throughout her life, Elira's mother had been a warrior, a relentless fighter, unyielding in the face of adversity. That indomitable spirit had carried her through countless battles, both seen and unseen, as she accepted pain and hardship as part of her existence. But now, as the final chapter of her life came to a close, it was time to lay down the armor and embrace the peace she had long yearned for a Paradise, as she had painted it in her mind, a place of absolute happiness.

Yet, what is Paradise but a creation of the mind, an illusion shaped by longing? Liv had spent her life seeking this elusive haven, imagining it as the end of all suffering, the fulfillment of her soul's deepest desires—a peace far more mysterious than euphoria. Indescribable!

Mourning was not the precise tribute Liv needed. Instead, she deserved to be released from the bonds of earthly suffering to find the ethereal serenity that awaited her. It was time to release her, to let her spirit soar beyond the confines of mortal existence.

As her mother entered this final phase, Elira, too, realized that she had to find the strength to let go. It was an ending and a beginning—a continuation of life's ever-turning cycle. She knew her mother's love would last forever, a timeless force that would never fade from her life. In response, she experienced fragments of memories, glimpses of a legacy.

Blurred by grief but lifted by hope, Elira finally let her mother find the peace she so deserved. She was ready to carry forward the lessons, the love, and the memories that would forever connect them. The time had come to move on from grief and embrace the profound beauty of a life well-lived, one that would resonate in the hearts of those left behind.

A new life was about to begin.

XVIII

<<I began to experience the most wonderful feeling. I couldn't feel a thing in the world except peace, comfort, ease - just quietness. I felt that all my troubles were gone, and I thought to myself, "Well how quiet and peaceful, and I don't hurt at all.">> ("Life After Life" by Raymond Moody)

A few years later, Elira began seeing herself, again and again, as a baby in Liv's arms. Strangely, she felt a powerful sense that her mother, from beyond, was sharing those very same emotions at the exact same moment. It was as if, in a parallel life, Liv truly was holding baby Elira. Perhaps it was a sign—a reminder that neither death nor time could break the sacred bond between mother and daughter.

Were they waking dreams, or just simple imagination? Elira didn't know, but she wanted to keep having the experience, to feel her mother's presence in any way possible. If she hadn't seen the image of herself as a baby before Teo's pregnancy, she might have thought that little Liv had triggered a memory in her mind.

Her life was beautiful. Her grief had softened into nostalgia; sometimes, she cried, but she never let Nick see. In truth, Elira had the perfect life.

She should have realized it when she first dreamed of Liv saying, "Ms. Doctor Death has healed me." A message beyond comprehension, a message that had come before and after her mother's passing into eternity. What clearer message could she have needed when, by definition, the word "doctor" means the one who heals you, and "Death" is the transition into the spirit, the end of physical pain?

Ms. Doctor, called Death, was the answer that Elira had to take advantage of, to understand that extreme mourning was no good, neither for those who mourned nor for those who had gone to the Divine Light.

After seeing those visions a few more times, Elira received a letter. She was surprised at first—who sends letters anymore? Everyone uses technology, so why would anyone bother to handwrite a letter? Then, she was shocked!

On the sender's square of the envelope, she read her mother's name and the return address, which simply said: "Heaven."

She opened it and started reading aloud as if hearing the words would make them more real:

My dear child,

I live in a splendid world that is impossible to describe with words. Perfection dominates the surroundings. It's beautiful, warm, pleasant, and full of light—ah, the light, my dear, dancing in fabulous colors. I want you to know that I don't feel any pain.

Sadness does not exist here, or at least I don't feel it. I don't even remember the disease, as if I were never sick. I don't have feelings that can upset me. It's Heaven!
What about you, my dear child? Why are you sad? How can you miss me when I'm always by your side? Don't you feel me? I know you do!

I know you dream about me and miss me, but all of this affects only you, my love; your grief won't bring me back, and I don't want to come back. I am at peace. I am living in supreme happiness, in all its forms, unimaginable to the living world. And knowledge, my child—here are the answers to all possible questions. Here lives God!

Put your mind to work, think, and live. The dead are not dead; they are alive beyond. There is life after life, and you must know that. There is a clock of the universe; there are rules from God. We must respect that and live our lives accordingly. I am sending this letter as proof, and you must stop suffering! Your place is there; mine is here! Continue to live, as the living do, and don't chase answers not yet allowed to you.

And if you still feel like doing things for me, do them. Bring me flowers at my tomb or leave them in places I used to love. Light a candle for more light, pray to God, and ask for an open mind. Be kind, give food to the poor in my name, and help those in need. Love the animals, and don't be cruel!
Oh, my dear, I almost forgot: please don't judge!

I love you, my sweet child; please love yourself, too!
The slow goodbye is not the end! The end is just another start!

With love from Heaven,
Mom

In reading "Mom," Elira woke up!

The End

ACKNOWLEDGEMENT

I would like to express my gratitude to my family, as well as to my friends Howard and Ann for their invaluable assistance.

I also wish to extend my thanks to all the friends who believed in me.